The System

A World Champion's Approach to Chess

Hans Berliner

5th World Correspondence Chess Champion

Developer of the Hitech Chess Machine/Program

First published in the UK by Gambit Publications Ltd 1999
Reprinted 2000, 2003
© Hans Berliner 1999

ISBN 1 901983 10 2

DISTRIBUTION:
Worldwide (except USA): Central Books Ltd, 99 Wallis Rd, London E9 5LN. Tel +44 (0)20 8986 4854 Fax +44 (0)20 8533 5821.
E-mail: orders@Centralbooks.com
USA: BHB International, Inc., 302 West North 2nd Street, Seneca, SC 29678, USA.
For all other enquiries (including a full list of all Gambit Chess titles) please contact the publishers, Gambit Publications Ltd, P.O. Box 32640, London W14 0JN, England. E-mail: info@gambitbooks.com
Or visit the GAMBIT web site at http://www.gambitbooks.com

Edited by Graham Burgess
Typeset by John Nunn
Printed in Great Britain by The Bath Press, Bath, Somerset

10 9 8 7 6 5 4 3

Gambit Publications Ltd
Managing Director: GM Murray Chandler
Chess Director: GM John Nunn
Editorial Director: FM Graham Burgess
German Editor: WFM Petra Nunn

Contents

Symbols and Abbreviations

+	check	∓	Black is slightly better
++	double check	∓	Black is much better
#	checkmate	−+	Black is winning
!!	brilliant move	Ch	championship
!	good move	OTB	over-the-board chess
!?	interesting move	CC	correspondence chess
?!	dubious move	1-0	the game ends in a win for White
?	bad move		
??	blunder	½-½	the game ends in a draw
+−	White is winning	0-1	the game ends in a win for Black
±	White is much better		
⩲	White is slightly better	(D)	see next diagram
=	equal position		

I am not Alone

Over 60 years ago Alekhine appreciated something that is still not common knowledge today.

After the moves:

1	d4	d5
2	c4	c6
3	♘c3	

"In my opinion this move gives White more chances of obtaining an opening advantage..."

3	...	dxc4
4	e4!	

"It is almost incredible that this quite natural move has not been considered by the so-called theoreticians. White obtains now an appreciable advantage in development, no matter what Black replies."

Alexander Alekhine, 1937

Bibliography

Books

Nimzowitsch, Aron; *My System*; Harcourt, Brace & Co., 1930
Kmoch, Hans; *Pawn Power in Chess*; David McKay & Co., 1959
Alekhine, Alexander; *My Best Games of Chess: 1924-1937*; Harcourt, Brace & Co., 1941
Kmoch, Hans; *Rubinstein's Chess Masterpieces*; David McKay Co., 1941
Réti, Richard; *Modern Ideas in Chess*; Dover Publications, Inc., 1960
Cheshire, Horace F.; *The Hastings 1895 Tournament*; Dover Publications, Inc., 1962
Adams, Weaver W.; *White to Play and Win*; David McKay & Co., 1945
De Groot, A.D.; *Thought and Choice in Chess*; Mouton & Co., 1965
Berliner, Hans; *From The Deathbed of 4. ♘g5 in the Two Knight's Defence*; From Berliner, 1998
Fine, Reuben; *The Ideas Behind the Chess Openings*; David McKay Co., 1943
Berliner, Hans & Messere, Ken; *Correspondence Chess World Championship*; British Chess Magazine, Ltd., 1971

Articles

Chase, W.G., & Simon, H.A.; *Perception in Chess*; Cognitive Psychology, 1973, no. 4, pp. 55-81
Berliner, H.; *The B* Tree Search Algorithm: A Best-First Proof Procedure*; Artificial Intelligence, 1979, vol. 12, no. 1, pp. 23-40

Foreword

What is 'The System' trying to do?

This is a book about how to play the chess opening. However, it is not a compendium of opening variations. You will not be able to look up your favourite lines here! However, you will be able to read about the ideas that should guide your play in most openings.

The System is a theory of how to integrate board control and development into a unified whole. At the start of a game of chess, White is ahead in development by half a move by dint of his being ahead 1 move after his turn, and 0 moves after Black has moved. The broad question is whether White can turn this small advantage to account as the game goes on. If White plays passively, Black will be able to mimic his moves, and after 7 to 10 moves, being to move will no longer constitute as much of an advantage as it does at the start of the game.

Therefore, White must do something to wring concessions from Black even as they are both trying to complete their development and compete for control of the board. This is what **The System** is about, and this book is about how to do this.

White's correct first move is 1 d4 because that controls three central squares while no other move controls more than two. Now Black has a choice of:

a) Competing in the centre by 1...d5, which leads to a struggle for control of the centre in which Black will inevitably be forced to make some small concessions in order to maintain his grip on the centre. **The System** maintains that these small concessions will result in White's advantage increasing.

b) Playing in the hypermodern style with 1...♘f6, which allows White to dictate the configuration in the centre (unless Black transposes to some line that could have come about after 1...d5). If White chooses wisely how to set up and control the centre, **The System** maintains that Black will never be able to attack it effectively. Thus, White will dictate the course of the game, resulting inevitably in a very strong attack in some sector where White has a large advantage in space.

The things that drive **System** play are board control and development. If White gets too far behind in development, or does not do enough to control the centre, Black will be able to dispose of White's half-move advantage in due time. We give a few examples of this. In fact, if White strays too far from the correct path, he may find himself at enough of a disadvantage in board control and development, so that Black may be the one that can apply **System** principles to defeat White. This kind of thing happens in the Berliner variation (10...e4!) of the Fritz Two Knight's Defence, and in many lines of the Rubinstein variation of the Four Knight's Game.

There seems to be some point where one side is far enough ahead to force his opponent to make concessions as discussed above. We believe that point also exists at the start of the game. The fact that Black has a very bad position after 1 d4 d5 2 c4 e6 3 ♘c3 ♘f6 4 cxd5 exd5 and after 1 d4 ♘f6 2 c4 g6 3 ♘c3 d5 certainly does not instil much faith in Black's ability to find a satisfactory defensive set-up. We have not as yet found any refutation of the Nimzo-Indian Defence, but are close. However, if the analyses of the Queen's Gambit Declined and the Grünfeld Defence are correct, then the future will certainly bring further refutations, and chess will be a solved game by the year 2030. Many will wring their hands at this, and hope that I am wrong. However, the enterprise of understanding how to play chess correctly is no different from any scientific enterprise that attempts to discover the structure of some domain. As such, interesting new results can be expected to keep pouring in. We here erect a framework for understanding and continuing this research.

The business of putting all this into a book has been very rewarding in terms of my personal understanding and ability to put my ideas into an understandable form. I wish to thank Dr John Nunn for his comments on Chapter 5.

Introduction

What is 'The System'?

This book is based upon the experiences of almost 50 years of studying, playing (over-the-board and in correspondence chess), and programming computers to play chess. We here present a theory that fulfils the scientific ideal of having principles based on experience. These principles have evolved slowly, as in the beginning there was nothing to build on.

We came to the problem of finding the best move for White in the original position with only the idea of the **Option** principle, first enunciated by W.W. Adams. We tried to apply it in the way he propounded, but it did not work. The fact that it did not work on 1 e4 did not discourage us. Later, the idea of applying it to 1 d4 appeared. As we got more experience with 1 d4 (which I had never played up to 1949), I began to realize its strength. 1 d4 leads to a board-control game, in which White, when playing properly, gradually takes over the board.

Success in certain openings allowed the beginning of the formulation of **System** principles; see Chapter 2. The number of principles and their precision gradually grew over the years. Although there are still things to learn, the **System** principles, as presented, form a formidable opus with which to attack chess. It is a theory which has now had a number of stunning successes against well-respected openings.

Very early on, we were able to deal with many variations of the Queen's Gambit Declined in a way that produced clear advantages against well-known defences. Also, the Modern Benoni opening was subjected to a new attack that was at the time not known, and can still not be found in the *Encyclopedia of Chess Openings*, despite the fact that it wins hands down. These lines can be found in Chapter 6 (p.119). The Benko Gambit, which has always seemed a bit dubious, was also refuted at this time, and this can also be found in Chapter 6 (p.124). Since 1990, I have finally found the clear refutation of the Grünfeld Defence after many false starts. And this is only a partial list of major defences that have been refuted.

You may ask "What is **The System**, and why should I pay attention to it?". The best answer I can give is that it presents a method of determining the best move for White, and given that each previous move was also correct, finding the best next move. That is quite formidable, if true. **The System** is a scientific theory; a theory of how to play chess. It is my theory only in so far as I discovered it. It is not ad hoc. It is as real as the theories of Gravitation and Evolution. It is as yet incomplete, but it has proven its mettle.

I liken **The System** to Mendeleev's Periodic Table of atomic elements. At the time this was formulated in the mid-nineteenth century, many elements were as yet unknown and the valences and atomic weights of others were in doubt. Yet, he was able to show a certain pattern for elements of valence +1, 0, and −1, and it was clear that there was a pattern here. Later, with the discovery of much missing data, the theory was confirmed and now is established fact. The families of elements are now known to have something to do with how many electrons are in their outer orbits; something that no one had a clue about at the time the initial observations were made.

In this little book, I present essentially the work of a lifetime. I have tried to get my computer Hitech to understand **The System**, however, with little success. Chess is mainly tactics. One must not lose material, nor pass up the opportunity to gain it. However, when there is little tactical to be done, one needs a strategy. **The System** is **the** strategy for playing the openings. However, things are not yet at the point where it is a completely mathematical theory (as Gravitation is). It is still rather qualitative, although some things have been formulated quite accurately (see Chapter 1) and tested in Hitech. With careful examination of the contents, I believe even the most die-hard sceptic will agree that we present excellent evidence that Black cannot achieve equality in such standard openings as:

a) The Grünfeld Defence;
b) The Queen's Gambit Declined;
c) The Benko Gambit;
d) The Modern Benoni.

Some History

How did all this come about? I have always been a theoretical type of person in that I observe, and then look for ways of explaining my observations. W. W. Adams was the first person I encountered who seemed to have a real theory of chess. Then, looking at Alekhine's games (in Alekhine's *My Best Games of Chess 1924-1937*), I could see the struggle for the initiative coming from the very first move. In fact, Alekhine played at least one game, shown partly in Chapter 7 (Game 3), where the play and notes show clearly that he understood much of what **The System** is about, but not quite enough. Later I studied the games of Rubinstein (in Kmoch's *Rubinstein's Chess Masterpieces*), who in just 6 months of self-study (according to fairly reliable folklore) transformed himself from a weak amateur to one of the top players in Poland. How could he have done this? He must have discovered some secret. Yes, he did, and I call it dynamism! He came to understand the dynamics of positions, especially endings. Here a rook & two pawns can be better than rook & three pawns if the two pawns are passed and connected, and far-advanced, sweeping everything in front of them. Also, a rook attacking isolated pawns was much more valuable than one defending such pawns. Such discernment of **dynamics** allowed Rubinstein to transform himself as a player. Dynamics is everywhere in chess. One bishop is always better than the other based upon dynamic considerations. Dynamics allows determining the value of pieces in the current environment and in those expected to be encountered in the future.

Later this dynamism was adopted by the hypermodern school that sought to control but not occupy the centre. However, their approach did not yield much unless the opponent willingly occupied the centre. This is what the 1940s Soviet resuscitation of the King's Indian Defence under Boleslavsky was all about. White occupies the centre, and now Black plays the hypermodern strategy. He eschews competing for the centre immediately, only to attack strongly later on.

The New Approach

However, the hypermodern strategy does not work for White. If he plays 1 ♘f3 as Réti did, which is certainly the flexible, hypermodern way to start, then Black need not compete in the centre. He can simply reply 1...♘f6 instead of 1...d5, and avoid creating a target. After 1...♘f6 Black can usually just copy White's moves and the road to equality is not too difficult. As the game progresses, the advantage of the move in a symmetrical position keeps getting smaller. So a different strategy is needed if White wants to obtain an advantage in the opening.

The **System** is the method for doing this. **The System** shows how effective board control can be made to work. White occupies and **controls** the centre, but in such a way that no counter-attack will succeed. If this is valid, and I believe it is, then chess is a long way toward being solved.

How to Read this Book

The System deals with how to play the opening with White. White starts out with a half-move advantage, and it is a question of whether this can be increased, or will it fade away. We believe it can be increased by putting the correct kind of pressure on Black, and we show how to do this.

In order to make good chess decisions in the opening and later, it is necessary to know what might lie ahead. One must know about:

a) How to determine the best location for each piece and how to get it there efficiently.

b) What kinds of advantages exist; how they compare in value, and how to determine which can be achieved.

c) Dynamic advantages which change the value of a piece or group of pieces from what they would be if one were merely to tally up their value. This subject has never been treated properly in the chess literature.

In this book, we attempt to walk the reader through the process of learning all this. Clearly, in such a small book, one cannot treat things to the fullest. However, I have tried diligently to deal with all subjects and give enough examples and other information, so that the interested reader can continue to develop his/her understanding. I have used as my model Fine's wonderful book *The Ideas Behind the Chess Openings*, which was inspirational for me. However, this book is much more than that. It deals with the openings as a whole domain for which complicated general ideas exist, rather than attempting to tell what to do in each opening.

Some Final Thoughts

Finally, when one constructs a theory, one cannot help but ponder its limitations. When it is a theory of Universal Gravitation, there are multitudinous events on which one can observe its correctness or lack thereof. This is because nature is nature. It has its rules and they do not change (we believe). However, when one theorizes about living things, and even worse about things made by living things, one must be very cautious about questions of correctness. Suppose there is something **The System** cannot deal with correctly (at present, we are quick to admit, there are several such things).

It is possible that the rules of chess are such that only some number of plausible-appearing defences to 1 d4 can be refuted. This is as if the laws of physics would not apply in certain parts of the Universe. This is certainly possible. We will not know until much more work on applying **The System** has been done.

Finally, I would like to thank Dr Peter H. Gould, wherever he may be. At a critical time in the early 1950s, Peter was my chess consultant. A master player himself, and a wonderful mathematician, we discussed **The System** from a theory point of view, rather than insisting that all variations be perfect. He saw my 'view' and agreed it was a theory. He also thought it was not too audacious to call it 'The System'. Now, of course, there is much more to it. Thank you, Peter, I hope you are well and happy.

1 The Basic Advantages[1]

In order to play chess well, one needs to know what one should be trying to do. There are certain advantages to try for, and one has to know how to recognize them and compute their value. Many books on chess tell you about certain of these advantages. However, we here attempt to go considerably more into detail than any other book I know of. This description of advantages is based on:

a) 30 years of top US over-the-board chess play;

b) The most outstanding record in world-class correspondence chess ever compiled;

c) Extensive experience in implementing these ideas for computer use.

Computers are very dumb at many things, but they follow directions beautifully. So what they accept as good, must be good.

Material

In any basic book on chess you will find the values of the pieces given as

Standard Piece Values	
Piece	**Value**
Pawn	1
Knight	3
Bishop	3
Rook	5
Queen	9

in the above table. This is convenient in teaching a beginner, but lacks the kind of precision needed to make meaningful decisions. For instance, using the above scale one could compute that a queen is worth 3 minor pieces (bishops or knights). Grandmaster experience has shown that three minor pieces are almost always much superior to a queen. Further, two minor pieces plus two pawns are almost always good compensation for a queen, and many times two minor pieces and one pawn is good enough. There are also trade-offs between the minor pieces and rooks, and the rooks and queen. One must understand how to make

---

1   There are certainly players who understand 90% of what is presented here. If they wish to take the risk of missing the other 10%, they could go on to Chapter 2, and possibly return here later.

decisions such as these in order to play a high level of chess.

System *Piece Values*	
Piece	**Value**
Pawn	1.0
Knight	3.2
Bishop	3.33
Rook	5.1
Queen	8.8

So, let me start by showing you the set of values that I have found most useful. These can be found in the table above. Immediately, I can hear you complain "But I am not a computer! How can I keep all these values in mind?" You really don't need to. You only need to understand the relationships among the values. For instance, now there should be no question that:

a) three minor pieces are about equal to ♕ + ♙;

b) two rooks are better than ♕ + ♙;

c) ♖ + ♗ are only a little bit worse than a queen;

d) ♘ + ♙ or ♗ + ♙ are usually considerably short of the value of a rook.

However, circumstances can alter evaluations. The worth of a piece can change mightily as a function of Pawn Structure. The straight-line pieces may gain up to 10% in value in wide-open positions, and lose up to 20% in blocked positions. The knight can gain up to 50% in value in blocked positions, and lose up to 30% in the corners and on the edges.

The value of a straight-line piece fluctuates in proportion to the number of squares on the board to which it can gain safe access. The value of the knight is determined by whether it has available any strong squares from which it can operate without fear of capture by equal or inferior pieces.

Chess positions may be classified as ranging from wide-open, to open, to average, to closed, to blocked. *Typical positions of each of the following types can be seen in the diagrams on the following page.*

a) A **Wide-open** position is one in which the pieces range freely without any significant obstruction by pawns. We have found that a good definition of wide-open is that at least two pairs of pawns have been exchanged, **and** there are no centre pawns abutting (blocking) each other. By centre pawns, we mean the d- and e-pawns.

b) An **Open** position is one in which at least one pair of centre pawns have been exchanged, **and** there are no blocked centre pawns.

c) An **Average** position is one in which there are no blocked centre pawns, and no pawns exchanged, or one in which one pair of pawns have

Wide-open position

Average position

Open position

Closed position

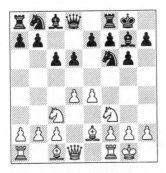

Average position

Blocked Position

been exchanged, but there is one centre block.

d) A **Closed** position is one in which there is one centre block, and there have been no pawns exchanged. Here centre block means the d- or e-file.

e) A **Blocked** position is one in which there are two adjacent centre blocks. This could be the c- & d-files, the d- & e-, or the e- & f-. Usually, the central pawns of one side tend to be on one colour of squares, while the pawns of the other side occupy the other colour. This makes for the so-called good and bad bishop. The bad one is blocked in activity by its own pawns. In such positions, one bishop of a pair may be worth 10% or more than the other.

The value of a piece can change as a function of Pawn Structure. We next discuss the essentials of Pawn Structure. Then beginning with the knight on p.21, we discuss the changing values of pieces. Again, bear in mind that it is not necessary to memorize these values. Rather, learn the general way that the data are sloped in this direction or that to indicate the type of changes in value that take place as a result of changes in pawn structure. Remember, a completely equal exchange of material practically never takes place, and knowing these values will help you to make favourable exchanges,

and avoid unfavourable ones. Also, you should be aware that all knowledge of this type was encoded as functions with sloping values that, in effect, said things such as "The value of a bishop increases as the openness of a position increases". We give the values just to give you a baseline for your understanding.

The Pawn

The Value of Pawns

As Philidor said "Pawns are the Soul of Chess", and this cannot be over-emphasized. Pawns affect the value of everything, and the whole **System** philosophy is based upon the idea of getting the good Pawn Structure that will make your position into a winning one.

First, let us look at simple things as shown in the first of the two tables on the following page. An average pawn is worth 1.0 in our scheme of things. However, d- & e-pawns are worth about 1.2, c- & f-pawns are worth about 1.1, b- & g-pawns are worth about 0.95, and h- & a-pawns are worth about 0.9. From this, it is already easy to see the reason for an old dictum "Always capture toward the centre".

These values apply during the opening and middlegame. In the late middlegame and ending, the values actually begin to reverse. As the amount of material on the board

		Values of Unpassed Pawns in the Opening			
		File of Pawn			
		(a,h)	(b,g)	(c,f)	(d,e)
Rank of Pawn	2	0.90	0.95	1.05	1.10
	3	0.90	0.95	1.05	1.15
	4	0.90	0.95	1.10	1.20
	5	0.97	1.03	1.17	1.28
	6	1 06	1.12	1.25	1.40

		Values of Unpassed Pawns in the Ending			
		File of Pawn			
		(a,h)	(b,g)	(c,f)	(d,e)
Rank of Pawn	2	1.20	1.05	0.95	0.90
	3	1.20	1.05	0.95	0.90
	4	1.25	1.10	1.00	0.95
	5	1.33	1.17	1.07	1.00
	6	1.45	1.29	1.16	1.05

diminishes, wing pawns gradually become more valuable than centre pawns (see the second of the two tables above). We have found through computer experimentation that pawns on any file are approximately equal in value when there are about 14 units of material each left on the board. After that, the value of wing pawns begins to increase slightly. The centre pawns have very few opposing pieces left to dominate, and the possibility of creating distant passed pawns begins to play an important role. Every piece exchange brings this moment closer, and should be kept in mind when selecting a move.

Further, a pawn can be part of a phalanx or be on its own. When it is part of a phalanx, we refer to it as **connected**. A pawn is connected when one of the following conditions is true:

1) It has one of its own pawns directly beside it on one of the adjacent files;

2) It can be protected in one move by the advance of one of its own pawns;

3) It can in one move place itself directly beside one of its own pawns without being lost.

Condition 3 above is a little tricky. If a pawn is behind its neighbours, and cannot immediately join one of them, it is called **backward**. Backward pawns are meaningful only on an open file, as otherwise they cannot be attacked frontally. A pawn may be behind its neighbour and physically able to join one of its neighbours but only at the cost of being lost. Such a pawn is connected, but backward. Backward pawns lose some of their mobility, and thus some of their value. However, that is about all one needs to know about them. Generally, they are to be avoided as they are almost as weak as isolated pawns.

If a pawn is not connected, it is **isolated**.

A pawn is **passed** when it can move forward all the way to the queening row without either:

a) Encountering an opponent's pawn;

b) Becoming exposed to capture by an opponent's pawn.

A pawn increases in value if:

a) It is passed;

b) It is connected;

c) It is advanced.

It decreases in value if it is:

a) Isolated;

b) Backward;

c) Multipled (Doubled or Tripled).

A pawn gains in value as it advances. Of course, it could be advancing straight into the jaws of death, but that is a tactical matter, and we assume that calculations will be made to assure the well-being of a pawn as it advances. A pawn's value does not increase much until it reaches the 5th rank, and then it increases its base value according to the table below which also shows the

gains for being passed, and passed & connected. These multipliers are to be applied to the base value of the pawn. However, as previously said, it is quite sufficient (unless you are a computer) just to understand the approximate change in value for each change of state.

Because pawns like to support each other and advance together, isolated and doubled pawns are to be shunned.

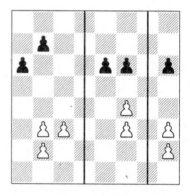

Different Kinds of Doubled Pawns

Doubled (multipled) pawns are a very complicated matter, and I know of no book that treats this subject

Value as a Pawn Advances				
		Isolated	Connected	Passed	Passed and Connected
Rank of Pawn	4	1.05	1.15	1.30	1.55
	5	1.30	1.35	1.55	2.3
	6	2.1	-	-	3.5

properly. The detriment caused by a doubled pawn is related to:

a) Its lack of mobility;

b) Its inability to perform its normal duties as a pawn;

c) The likelihood that it can never be exchanged for an opponent's normal pawn.

In the right-hand side of the above diagram is seen the worst kind of doubled pawn. It is almost worthless as the only value the pair has over a single pawn is that extra square(s) are controlled by the multipled pawns. Such a doubleton is worth approximately 0.33 and further such multipled pawns are worth only 0.2.

In the central portion of the diagram is seen a more usual situation in which the doubled pawn has some defensive potential, since the opposing pawns in that sector cannot advance without undoubling the pawns. However, the pawns are isolated and can be easily attacked. They are very weak; here the back doubleton is worth about 0.5.

The left-hand side shows a still more usual situation. Here the doubled pawns are part of a phalanx facing opposing pawns on adjacent files. They may be dissolvable with the aid of pieces. If, for instance, a white light-squared bishop existed it may be possible to play b4, b5 and dissolve the doubleton. Here the doubled b-pawn is worth 0.75. If the black a-pawn were on the c-file, it would not be possible to dissolve the doubled b-pawn, and it would be worth only 0.5.

So the detriment that a multipled pawn causes is a function of how many pawns are encumbered that way and whether any of them can be dissolved. Every undissolvable doubled pawn loses at least 50% of its value. However, one must be very careful in making the assessment of dissolvability. If there is some doubt, a reduction of 30% is more proper.

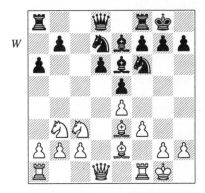

The d6-pawn is backward

Isolated and backward pawns also lose some of their value, but mainly while they are on the 2nd to 4th ranks. Here, a so-encumbered pawn loses about 15% of its value. However, while isolated pawns can at best hope to control some meaningful territory, a backward and connected pawn frequently poses a real threat to the opponent, as its advance can 'free' the whole position. In the above diagram, if Black can achieve the ...d5 advance his position is immediately freed.

The Use of Pawns

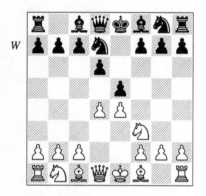

**White controls d5;
Black does not control d4**

Being able to use your pawns effectively is, after mastery of tactics, the most important aspect of playing good chess. To control a square means that a unit could legally capture an opponent's piece if it were on that square. As pawns are the least valuable unit, they can terrorize the other pieces. Thus, pawns can and should be used to control the board. Pieces can help in control but are definitely secondary to pawns. Square control comes in several different varieties:

a) Absolute Control (square, myside) – myside has a pawn controlling square, and the opponent does not.

b) General Control (square, myside) – neither player has a pawn controlling square, but my side can put a minor piece there safely, and opponent cannot.

c) Disputed control (square) – neither player can put a minor piece on square safely.

In the above diagram White exercises absolute control over d5 and f5, and Black exercises absolute control over d4 and f4. White exercises general control over g5, c4 and many other squares, while Black exercises general control over no squares. If White were to play c3, this would result in disputed control over d4. However, if a pawn is safely occupying a square, it is not terribly important if the opponent has absolute control, as long as the pawn can safely remain there. This is a very important distinction, upon which much of the opening theory in **The System** is based. If the pawns at d4 and d6 were removed from the board, and the c2-pawn were to advance to c4, then the absolute control of d4 by Black would be a serious matter, as White could not put a pawn or piece there, and Black could eventually occupy it with a piece.

Clearly, it is best to control squares absolutely. However, the opponent is also interested in controlling squares, so many squares will be under disputed control. However, White should play in such a way as never to give up absolute control over an important square that can no longer be occupied by own pawn. This would be a major roadblock in the plan to take over the board.

It is the fervent desire of both sides to control as much territory as possible, especially in the centre. As will be further explored in Chapter 2, White should have a very strong desire to control his side of the board, especially the centre squares e4, d4, c4 and f4.

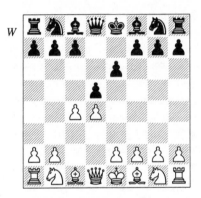

Lever Action – the Pawn at c4

Pawns, besides being able to control key squares, can also attack the opponent's pawn phalanxes. The attack that Kmoch (in *Pawn Power in Chess*) calls the **lever** is very useful in attacking pawn structures. An example of a lever, where a pawn attacks a pawn phalanx from the side, is seen in the above diagram. Here the white c4-pawn is threatening to

eventually trade itself off for the more valuable centre pawn on d5. In the meantime, it is creating tension in the centre.

The thing that distinguishes **The System** most from any other proposed way of playing chess, is its strong emphasis on board control. This will be explained in detail in Chapter 2.

The Knight

It is well known that the knight is strongest in the centre of the board and weakest at the edges, especially the corners. However, there are many things about knights that are not that obvious. A knight benefits greatly from closed and blocked pawn structures, to the point where if the position is going to remain closed, it is much to be preferred to have a knight rather than a bishop. To see that this is seldom the case, just think how easy it would be to play ♗g5 after Black has played ...♘f6 and take off the knight. If that were good in general, chess would be a different game. But in some very blocked positions, it may be good.

It is very important to have an understanding of how the degree of closedness of a position affects the value of a knight. Usually, knights and bishops are in direct competition since exchanges of knight for bishop and vice versa are always in the wind. So, as a position gets more open, the knight's value wanes and the bishop's increases. As a position becomes more closed, the opposite happens.

Good Knight Placements

One other thing is very important for knights. Since they do not run very fast, they benefit greatly from freedom of being attacked. So a knight in the centre that cannot be attacked by an opposing pawn is very strong, as for instance in front of an isolated opposing pawn. Also, even when free from future pawn attacks, a knight does not want to be driven away by a major piece that is threatening to capture it. From this point of view it is very important to have anchoring points. An anchor is provided on a square guarded by one's own pawn, and this essentially assures the knight life in that location. Nimzowitsch presented a wonderful treatment of the concept of 'outpost' in his book *My System*. Outposts can exist anywhere a pawn can support a fellow knight while no opponent's pawn can harass it. In the left-hand side of the above diagram is a knight well placed in front of an isolated c5-pawn; on the right is a knight anchored at e4 by the f3-pawn and free from any attacks by pawns or major pieces.

The Straight-line-moving Pieces

All the straight-line-moving pieces have an increase in activity and therefore value as the number of pawns on the board diminishes. These pieces become much more powerful in the ending. So while a knight and two (undistinguished) pawns may be approximate equal to or better than a rook in the middlegame, they will be definitely inferior in the ending. When in possession of a bishop versus a knight, it is definitely correct to exchange some pawns to enhance the mobility of the bishop.

The Bishop
However, a bishop has some other interesting properties. Since it is confined to the squares of one colour, it usually needs some other pieces to cooperate with in order to bring out its best performance. This may be other straight-line pieces that can move on the opposite colour, or

they may be pawns. Bishops and pawns collaborate beautifully as long as the pawns are mobile. The pawns can be set up to control one colour and the bishop the other. On the other hand, bishop and knight seldom collaborate well. Just see how difficult it is to mate with bishop and knight against a lone king, when neither side has any pawns.

There is one feature of bishop existence that a good player must be able to master, and that is the notion of bishop badness. As already mentioned, the bishop gets worse as the pawn structure gets more closed. However, some closed structures are really deadly for a bishop. These have own blocked pawns on the same colour squares as the bishop. This brings on the so-called **bad bishop**, and it comes in various degrees of badness.

A bishop can be bad according to the number of its own pawns (especially centre pawns) that are on its colour.

In the following diagram we see a bishop that is almost useless. It has no targets to attack, and its own pawns are largely on the same colour as the bishop. This dooms the piece to complete passivity. White can win rather easily by playing f3, followed by g4. To meet this Black must either:

a) Play ...hxg4, fxg4, which creates a potential passed h-pawn that

A very bad bishop

will require the attention of the black king, whereupon the white knight penetrates decisively on the queenside; or

b) Play 1 f3 ♚e7 2 g4 ♞f6 3 gxh5 gxh5 whereupon 4 ♞b5 a6 5 ♞d6 wins rather easily.

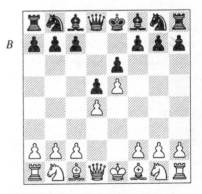

The black c8-bishop is very bad

In this diagram, we see a somewhat different setting. The black c8-bishop is bad because it is inside its own pawn-chain, and that chain is fixed in place on the same colour as itself. If it could get to a6, most of its problems would be solved. It could then exchange itself for White's good f1-bishop or possibly a knight. On the other hand, the white c1-bishop is only a little bad. This stems from the fact that it has a reasonably good scope but will be hampered in its activity by its own pawns in the centre. Meanwhile, the white f1-bishop is the star performer as it has plenty of targets and is not hampered at all. The black f8-bishop is an average bishop. It can get targets, and is not hampered by its own pawns. However, we deduct 0.1 pawns worth from the value of all bishops in blocked positions, and add 0.1 for the value of all knights. Further, bishops that have one or more of their own centre pawns fixed on their own colour suffer further deductions, as do bishops that are trapped behind their own pawn-chain, as is the c8-bishop. So, in such a position, the knights are worth 3.30 and the best bishop is only worth 3.23.

Again, I only want to emphasize the factors that go into evaluating a bishop, and not urge anyone to pay much attention to the actual numbers; only the approximate magnitude. This will allow you to see the advantage of fixing a pawn-chain or avoiding this. Clearly, one should try to avoid getting one's own bishops to be bad, but it is a good strategy to so encumber one's opponent's bishops.

Further, it is almost always the case that one bishop is better than the other, and when considering exchanging, it is clear the worse bishop should be exchanged. Also, by having a clear idea of just how good or bad a knight or bishop is in a given situation, it is easier to make decisions about whether to exchange one for another.

We have not mentioned the value of a piece due to its location. It is clear that bishops on good diagonals are worth additional value, possibly as high as 0.15, and knights on good centre posts from which they cannot be dislodged are worth from 0.15 to 0.5 additional points in value on the above scale of values. Understanding these issues is worth a lot in formulating strategy.

The Rook

Rooks are sleepers in the early stages of the game. They seldom play a meaningful role until at least one open file exists. However, there are occasional opportunities by means of a4-a5 or h4-h5 for White to open a file while the rook is still on its original square. Such opportunities should not be ignored, and the decision to castle frequently involves giving up such chances. One other thing should be noted about rooks on open files. In many positions it may be possible to open a file and place as many as two rooks upon it. However, this strategy may be useless if the opponent controls the entry squares on the 6th, 7th, and 8th ranks with pawns and minor pieces. This happens in the Ruy Lopez closed positions, and also in variations of the King's Indian Defence, to name just two.

A very powerful rook (c7)

pawns, as in the diagram directly above.

The Queen

No chess piece has undergone more of a change of appraisal of its value in the last two centuries than the queen. It is just not true that a queen is worth more than rook, bishop and pawn. In the eighteenth and nineteenth centuries almost all games began with 1 e4, and wide-open positions were the norm. In such situations there are usually a number of undefended targets, and the queen, with its many attacking rays, can take advantage of such situations.

However, nowadays the average position is much more closed, and the value of the queen diminishes accordingly. In positions that are basically closed, it is possible to sacrifice the queen for two minor pieces and obtain a positional advantage if

A very powerful knight

Finally, as mentioned earlier, rooks increase in value as pawns are exchanged. This is most noticeable when comparing the value of a knight with that of a rook. In certain blocked positions, such as the diagram above, a knight can be as strong as a rook. However, as pawns are exchanged, one can eventually reach positions where a rook will make mincemeat of knight & two

the minor pieces are well placed, and cannot be driven away. In such situations, if the queen cannot find any targets, it will usually be at a disadvantage.

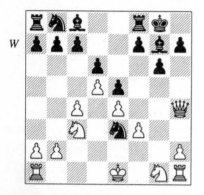

White to play; Black's Two Pieces + pawn are better than a queen

♖ + ♘ dominate ♛

Even in less closed positions, one important thing must always be kept in mind about the queen. It is powerful on offence, but it is only **one unit** on defence. Thus, two enemy pieces can gang up on a target pawn that cannot be defended by a pawn, and thus outnumber the queen's one defensive ray. The above facts have contributed greatly to a change in understanding of the queen's value. For instance, in the first diagram above Black has sacrificed his queen for two bishops & pawn without obtaining any attacking chances. However, his pieces are dominant, and White's queen can do little. Black stands considerably better. Also, in the second diagram above, White's queen is just a bystander while Black will pick off White's vulnerable pawns one by one.

Positional Advantages

King Safety

It is clear that king safety is very important. If the king is not safe, then sacrifices of material can open further breaches to win material and/or produce a mate.

There is little I can add to what is found in any good book about the subject of king safety. In our computer work it has become clear that if there is only one pawn available to shelter the king, then the best pawn is the central one of the triad, the b- or g-pawn. Also, one can have a

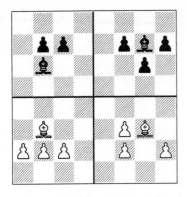

Bishops enhancing king safety

weak pawn phalanx around the king, if one has board control over that area. One subject that is seldom discussed is how pieces other than pawns can shelter the king. It is clear that an f3-knight is useful in defending a white king's castled position. However, bishops can also be used in king safety, especially when the pawn structure has been ruptured. Thus, all the positions in the above diagram show ways in which a bishop can augment king safety.

Pawn Structure

The System detests isolated pawns, and you should too. It is not so much that isolated pawns have to be defended by pieces; it is much more that the squares in front of an isolani can no longer be attacked by a pawn. **The System** favours a board control strategy, and when there are important squares that can no longer be controlled, the strategy has probably failed. Isolated pawns may be all right if they are passed; particularly if they are centre pawns and have advanced beyond the 4th rank. Isolated pawns are also not a serious disadvantage if they are a- or h-pawns because the squares in front of them are not very important. Side-by-side pawns on the 4th rank such as on d4 and e4, or c4 and d4 are very good. They control a significant part of the board, and as such are worth much more than they amount to individually.

Pawn structure is very nicely described in Kmoch's wonderful book *Pawn Power in Chess*. It does not deal very quantitatively with the value of pawns, but it does describe pawn interactions extremely well.

As already discussed, pawn structure significantly affects the value of individual pieces. In blocked positions, a knight is probably more valuable than the worse of a bishop pair. So one should manage pawn structure to suit the pieces, and vice versa. There are several examples of this in this book.

It is frequently possible in a position of **average** openness, to make decisions that affect whether the future pawn structure will be **closed**, **blocked** or **open**. Such decisions should be made with the pieces on the board in mind. If there is some possible exchange pending, it is good to go for the pawn structure that favours what will be left. There are frequently opportunities to exchange a bishop for knight, and then partially close or block the position. This is like enhancing the value of the remaining pieces, and is a distinct advantage that should be sought out when possible. The same kind of thing happens in bishop vs knight situations, where the side with the bishop should be interested in opening the position up, and exchanging centre pawns for wing pawns, while the side with the knight should try to keep the pawn structure as closed as possible and avoid pawn exchanges.

Board Control

The thing that distinguishes **The System** from other approaches to the chess opening is its emphasis on board control. Chess is a struggle that involves all the pieces. Historically, good players beginning with Morphy learned to get their pieces out early in the game to be prepared for the struggle. However, as sophistication set in, the best players began to realize that just getting a piece out was not enough; one should try to get it to its best location. The hypermoderns realized that sometimes a piece is extremely well placed on its original square, as

for instance the c8-bishop is in the King's Indian Defence.

If one side controls most of the important squares in the centre, it will be increasingly difficult for the other side to develop his pieces to meaningful locations. Of course, there is a trade-off here. One cannot exclusively make square-controlling pawn moves without falling far behind in development. If one gets far enough behind, the other side can make sacrifices, and break the controlling bind to its advantage. So White must combine the strategy of board control with a certain amount of development to avoid getting too far behind.

Board Control is the most important advantage, assuming the king is secure. The hypermoderns built their theories on how to control and attack the centre. However, we will show much new ground to be mastered. The most important area of the board to control are the four central squares, and secondary to these are the squares c4, c5, f4, f5 that surround them. One important facet of board control is colour complexes. One should be very careful in exchanging a bishop, as this could be the primary defender of the squares of its colour. True, pawns can also defend those squares, and sometimes even other pieces. However, the bishop is primary and to exchange a bishop that is guarding important squares of its colour, can be foolhardy.

White is half a move ahead to begin with and can use this advantage either to make a controlling move which does not increase his development, or to make a developing move. Hopefully, he can do both at the same time. In any case, he should be careful to preserve his options, so that important future controlling moves will not be blocked. This is one of the most important principles in **System** philosophy.

The major thing that distinguishes **System** philosophy from previous opening theories, is the firm commitment for White to control the centre on his side of the board; i.e. the squares d4 and e4. Historically, White has been content to just get his pieces out, and then expect active play.

However, **The System** does not want to give up e4 to Black unless White gets something concrete in return. To this end, the move f3 frequently comes in after White has already established his grip on d4, and now wishes to control e4 also. A move such as f3 in the opening could very well be made instead of developing a piece, in the hope that the board control achieved thereby is worth the loss of time. However, as previously mentioned, White must be careful about how far behind in development this makes him. We show a number of examples of this critical concept.

Development: The Placement of the Pieces

Piece Placement is well covered in classical chess texts. The hypermoderns discovered that the classical notions of piece placement were not completely adequate to evaluate many positions. We build on this in our theories, as we describe how to reach the maximum dynamic potential of a position. Also, classical notions of **Development** seem rather antiquated now. Yes, one must get the pieces out; however, not slavishly but rather in a very organized way that balances the need for getting the pieces out while at the same time asserting one's influence on the board.

Concern with development is, together with board control, the primary concern of **The System**. One must try to get the pieces out, but only to their best squares, and with the aim of controlling the board. So how does one improve upon the slavish development ideas of the Classical School of Chess?

There are two ways of looking at development:

a) The Classical view is: How many pieces has each side developed, counting 1 point for each one and then taking the difference between the development of each side.

b) The Dynamic view is: How many pieces still need to be developed, counting −1 point for each one and then taking the difference between the lack of development of each side.

According to Classical ideas, 1 unit of development is assigned to each piece that has left the back rank. Castling gets 1 unit, and a rook on an open or semi-open file also gets 1 unit. However, we have found that this system leaves a lot to be desired. There are situations in which a piece on the back rank is as well developed as it can possibly be. Further, there are many issues about pawns being developed (on which Classical authors differ), and whether to give more than 1 unit for (say) a knight on d4, or for castling. We use a different system, of my own design, which is both simpler and more accurate in assessing development.

In the Dynamic method, the development count is −10 for each side at the start. From this we count down:

a) 1 point for each piece that is in a good developed position (including those that have not moved yet!);

b) 1 for having the king in a safe position;

c) 1 for each of the two centre pawns advanced beyond their original squares;

d) 1 extra point for a knight in the centre, as long as it cannot be driven

away, and White has already developed over half his pieces.

A rook is considered developed if the pawn of its own side in front of it is advanced at least to the 5th rank (or gone altogether). While castling gets 1 unit of development, one is well advised to heed the maxim **Castle if you must, or if you want to, but not because you can!** The point is that there are positions where the decision of where to put the king is best postponed until the character of the position becomes very clear. There are many examples in this book where the white king stays in or near the centre because that is the best place for it.

The question of what is the best location for a piece is frequently touched on in this text. However, it can be quite difficult to determine whether a piece is 'developed'. I have given the rules and obvious exceptions above. We have already mentioned the black c8-bishop in the King's Indian Defence that participates from here as well as from potentially any other square. However, how about a move such a ♔f1 to remove the king to what is considered the best location in the position (this move could also be forced). Is this a developing move?

The easiest way to look at these problems is simply to count **What still needs to be done?** If certain pieces are not participating, then they are not developed, and should get a −1. Pieces that appear to be optimally located (even if they have not moved yet) are considered developed. Also, rooks on their original square that are on an open file, or on one that is threatening to be opened are not in need of development. If a rook is 'undeveloped' but has no good location to go to, then this is still some unfinished business, but not something that must be attended to right away. The same could be true of a queen.

One other aspect of this method which is more accurate than the classical way is in dealing with sacrificed pieces. In the classical scheme a sacrificed piece is **undeveloped**; i.e. it does not have a development count associated with it. However, presumably it was sacrificed on purpose to gain in development of some other advantage. Therefore, it is foolish to reduce the development count because of its absence, rather than to think of how many units of development are required to bring those pieces left on the board to their optimal location.

There is one other thing about development that is important. The mere difference in development of the two sides is not always indicative of what is going on. For instance, if one side has a development count of −6, and the other has −4, then the difference is 2 units. The same would

be true if one side had a count of −2, and the other a count of 0. In the latter case, one side is completely developed and ready for action, while in the former, both sides still have a way to go. Clearly, if one side has completed development he is in a position to start immediate action, and this can be very dangerous to the opponent. In the first example, the difference in development is the same, but the application of this difference is still a few moves away. So some ratio of completion of development would be useful. Since the attack usually starts once one side has completed his development, the closer one side is to completing his development, the better is his position.

When considering a pawn sacrifice for gain of development, the standard rule of "A pawn is worth three tempi" is a good one. However, be very wary of winning a pawn by giving 3 tempi. That is seldom wise in the opening.

Mobility

Everyone prizes mobility (and it is important in every game I know of). However, in chess it seems to be only a good tie-breaker, all other things being equal. For instance, which is better:

a) A rook that can move to 10 different squares, or

b) A rook that can only move to 8, but is attacking a backward pawn?

Clearly, the latter is better, which shows that pure mobility (the ability to move to a square) is not a good enough notion. One must consider what squares, and what is on those squares, and how central they are, etc.

All this shows that the above notions must be merged into some larger whole to get a full appreciation of a position. Since mobility is frequently tied to such other notions as whether a piece is in a defensive position, it is usually satisfactory to ignore it. That is what is done in the best chess programs.

2 The System Principles

Introduction

There is a great deal of discussion among top chess players about certain basic aspects of the game. Everyone is agreed that White, by virtue of having the first move, stands better in the starting position. We can characterize the fact that White makes the first move as White being half a move ahead, as that is what it amounts to. He is one move ahead after having moved, and no moves ahead after Black has moved. Thus, on average, he is half a move ahead. The basic question is: "Can he maintain and/or increase this lead, or must it be dragged down to equality, assuming both players are making best moves?"

While every player would prefer to be White at the start of a game, almost all players believe White's advantage is insufficient for a win. It is assumed that mistakes by Black are more severely punished than those by White since they add to an already existing inferiority. However, all GMs will be quick to point out that the advantage of the first move is **temporary**, and one cannot expect to be able to sustain it[1].

The idea that chess is a draw comes from the results of hundreds of thousands of games. Of course, it is not possible to tell whether White has a winning advantage or not, so one relies on statistics about outcomes. However, such statistics include all sorts of games: games in which the weaker player plays White, and games where even the stronger player as White plays without the very best plan. Even then, of the decisive games, White wins about 60%.

What should White be trying to do at the start of a game of chess? The books will tell to get your pieces out so they can participate in the fight. However, there is a lot more to it than that. **The System** is knowledge distilled from successful practice of opening play. It dictates that

---

1   In the last 30 years, two games in which the starting player was always thought to have a strong advantage have been mathematically proven to be wins for the first player. These games are CUBIC (three-dimensional 4x4x4 tic-tac-toe/noughts and crosses), and Connect 4, a game played on 7 vertical columns.

development and **board control** are to be very closely tied in the strategy of making opening moves. In this chapter, we assert the Principles of **System** play.

Such principles allow us to determine why one first move for White is better than any other. Currently, top players believe that how you start is a matter of taste. However, all players agree that if there is a best first move, it must be either 1 d4 or 1 e4. Players who count on slam-bang tactics will usually prefer 1 e4, while positional players prefer 1 d4. Could it be that one of these two moves is actually better than the other? We believe that is the case. Read on, and you will find out which one and why.

How Can Useful Principles be Developed?

There is a story told about Emanuel Lasker, the long-time World Chess Champion around the turn of the century. It seems that in his travels Lasker once stopped in a small German town and went to the local chess club. There, he introduced himself and asked to play the strongest player. He was soon able to determine that the fellow he was playing was quite weak, and so took the liberty of putting his queen where it could be captured. After some thought, his opponent made a move on the other side of the board.

"Why didn't you capture my queen?" inquired Lasker. "What! And double my pawns in front of the castled king?" came the immediate reply.

What makes this story funny is that everyone realizes a queen is worth far more than doubled pawns in front of the king. And since everybody can distinguish the disparity, the unknown opponent's behaviour is laughable. However in everyday practical chess, there are thousands of much more difficult comparisons of advantages and potential advantages that must be made. We have striven to show the important advantages in Chapter 1. We now rely on this information in defining a scheme for achieving as many of these advantages as possible.

In the sections that follow, we present first the **System** principles, and then give examples of how they work.

The System Principles

Principle 1: Tactics is King

Everything White does must be tactically sound. This means material must be conserved. However, it also means that:

a) White should not disregard other principles just to win a pawn.

b) White should be willing to sacrifice a pawn if there is a gain in several tempi, and/or it furthers the achievement of important strategic goals that cannot be achieved otherwise. In general, three tempi are worth a pawn, but this does not mean that it is good strategy to win a pawn and give two tempi. Moves must conform to the Principles, and White should not be distracted by winning a pawn, if it derails the basic strategy.

However, gains of material greater than a pawn should always be seriously considered. To give a ridiculous example: after 1 d4 d5 2 c4 dxc4 3 e4 ♕xd4??, the correct move is 4 ♕xd4 even though this develops the queen prematurely. Captures of pieces should routinely be considered as the best **System** move, until it becomes clear that they are not.

As illustrated above, White should not slavishly make **System** moves when there are tactical considerations. **The System** dictates which moves to select under **strategic** conditions. Under no circumstances should one ignore the win of a piece, or ignore the threat to one's own piece for **System** reasons. However, if you are in a **System** position, it will seldom if ever be necessary to retreat unless some material has already been won. Here we are not including actions such as a threat to a piece by a pawn that allows retreat to an almost-as-good location, and may have come at the expense of Black weakening his pawn structure.

For instance, after a move such as ...h6 by Black, threatening a g5-bishop, its retreat to h4 should not be thought of as a retreat. The white bishop retains its position on the d8-h4 diagonal, and ...h6 may very well be a weakening move. In any case, it does not contribute to Black's development. Most of the time, if faced with an apparent need for retreat, think carefully, because there may be some **System** idea that avoids the retreat. Examples of this can be found in the games of Chapter 7.

Principle 2: Piece Location

Each piece has an optimum location, and possibly several near-optimum locations. It is important to determine these locations early in the play, and try to get each piece to its optimal location. Optimal locations are defined by the considerations of Chapter 1.

Principle 3: Development

Pieces should be brought to their optimal location by moving each piece **only once**, although in the case of knights it may be permissible to move a knight twice if the second move is to a centre square (which it clearly could not have reached in one move). However, such moves should be postponed until most of the other pieces have been developed. In a strict sense, pawns are not developed, but rather are positioned as control units in the fight for the centre. White should try to make only moves of the central pawns, and each only once (other than captures and recaptures). In general, if no better location for a piece exists on its side of the board, then it is developed.

The sub-principles below cover certain situations that may exist:

a) Do not make defensive moves unless they are part of your development plan. White has the initiative, and the only way to maintain it is to keep doing aggressive things.

b) Don't make a capture that aids the opponent's development.

c) Consider the possibility that a piece may be well placed on its original square. An h1-rook could be part of a kingside attack with h4-h5.

d) Castle if you want to or if you must, but not because you can.

e) Don't exchange bishop for knight unless you get some noticeable advantage in return.

always be accomplished, White must decide whether to strive for occupation, or just to deny the opponent the use of these squares by controlling them with pawns. If the opponent is occupying the centre with a pawn, it should be attacked by a wing pawn lever; e.g. a black d5-pawn should be attacked by c4 (see Kmoch's *Pawn Power in Chess*). If the opponent is not occupying the centre, White should strive to take it over. Do not attack a mobile pawn with a pawn, as it is not a fixed target for attack.

White's side of the board belongs to him. The other side is to be taken over. If Black encroaches on White's side of the board, he must be immediately challenged. If Black can effectively position a piece on White's half of the board, it is safe to say White has misplayed the **System** strategy. He should never give up control of the important squares on his side of the board. And he should try to take over as many important squares as possible on Black's side of the board.

Principle 4: Board Control: Attack and Control the Centre

The centre should be attacked by pawns supported by pieces. It is ideal to have pawns on the two central squares on White's side of the board: d4, and e4. Since that cannot

Principle 5: Options

The **Option Principle** states: **make the move (develop the piece) which does the least to reduce your options to make other important moves**. When there are several pieces that can be developed, move the one for which the Optimal Placement is most clear. This is a generalization of Lasker's rule "knights before bishops". Usually a bishop has more good locations to choose from than a knight, so develop the knight first. However, the **System** options principle is much more general. It frequently encourages the non-movement of a piece that is already well placed on the back rank. It may also discourage castling, if the rook is well placed for an attack.

The Option Principle also prohibits making a move that blocks a friendly piece from reaching its optimal location. For instance, the sequence 1 d4 d5 2 ♘c3 is prohibited even though c3 is the best location for the b1-knight. It blocks the advance c4, and that is essential for attacking the centre pawn on d5. Likewise, 2 e3 is prohibited, as it keeps White from developing his c1-bishop to certain good locations, and also commits the pawn to a one-square advance when it may be possible later to advance it two squares to a better location.

Under the Option Principle, there is always at least one move that is crying out to be played before other moves. In the rare case where there is more than one such move, the decision must be made based on other factors. For instance, after the moves 1 d4 d5 2 c4 e6 3 ♘c3 ♘f6 is it better to play 4 ♗g5 or 4 cxd5? In Chapter 4, we show which one is correct based upon complex reasoning. Later in this chapter (p.43), we present extensive examples of the Option Principle at work.

Principle 6: Response Pairs

In certain openings, there may be several pieces that are ready at the moment to move to their optimal location. The question is "Which one should be moved next?". In most such situations, the opponent has plans of his own. This may require that at its optimal location, a white piece also perform some defensive duties. By observing Black's build-up, White can determine which of these optimal moves must be invoked next, or whether any defence is needed and White can ignore the requirement.

Thus, if Black's move A1 requires the response A2 by White, and Black's move B1 requires B2 by White, there is a simple rule for deciding which move should be selected next. Thus, the game could continue:

a) 1...B1 2 B2 A1 3 A2; or

b) 1...A1 2 A2 B1 3 B2.

Either way, the same position arises, but with White countering Black's threat correctly in each variation.

So the **Response Pairs** principle states **there may be openings in** which certain white moves are required as responses to black moves. This will result in some pairings of the type: black move → white reply. This principle shows that the preferred order of developing pieces may be dependent upon what Black is trying to do.

Principle 7: Transpositions

The **Transposition Rule** states "Do not allow Black to reach some position that is better than what he could have reached in another known **System** line leading to the same position." Consider the position reached after 1 d4 d5 2 c4 e6 *(D)*.

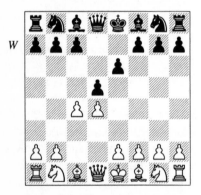

The question here arises which of several moves is the correct **System** move. Potential candidates include the move 3 cxd5. We now show why 3 cxd5 cannot possibly be correct, using the Transposition Rule.

It is possible to reach the standard position in the Queen's Gambit Declined by more than one route. Thus, after 1 d4 ♘f6 2 c4 e6 it would not be possible to play 3 cxd5 as there is no d5-pawn. On the other hand, if the game continues 3 ♘c3 d5 then the capture 4 cxd5 is possible. So if cxd5 is correct on the 4th move in this position, it cannot possibly be correct on move 3 before the knights have come out. To cement this, one could enquire what possible detriment could come out of playing 3 cxd5. The answer is that White may be in a position to wring another concession (see below) from Black by getting him to block his f-pawn with ...♘f6. On the other hand, 3 cxd5 exd5 allows the c8-bishop out without having wrung out any more concessions.

Principle 8: Resolution – Don't Prematurely Relinquish Concessions Gained

The **resolution** principle states that if there is some issue to be resolved (such as central tension) wait as long as possible to resolve it, but it must be resolved before moving on to the next stage (such as attacking a pawn that is already under tension). By failing to resolve the tension and instead attacking a mobile target, White will make it difficult to threaten this point later on. In essence, **resolution fixes the target at a time when this** is appropriate, because no more concessions can be wrung out.

Principle 9: When there are no Threats

If the opponent has absolutely no threats, and there are no excellent developing moves to be made, attack a fixed target or make a space grab. The point of this is to deal with those positions where Black is essentially waiting for White to commit to a premature attack. If Black makes no move that qualifies for a response under the **Response Pairs** principle, then White is free to do as indicated above.

In Summary

By observing all the Principles above, White will be able to develop his position smoothly to increase the advantage of the first move. The reason for the increase is that Black will be forced to make small concessions in order to meet White's plans. For instance, after the moves 1 d4 d5 2 c4 *(D)* Black is faced with:

   a) Giving up the centre with 2...dxc4;

   b) Defending the centre with 2...e6, which blocks in his queen's bishop;

   c) Defending the centre with 2...c6, which takes away the best square of the b8-knight;

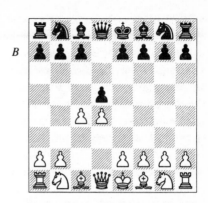

   d) Other, less popular, moves that also make concessions.

In this way **The System** wrings small advantages from Black.

How did these System Principles Arise?

I first met Weaver ('White to Play and Win') Adams back in 1946. His theories, though looked upon with scorn by most top chess players, made an immediate and lasting impression on me. Weaver W. Adams was the first person I met who actually had theories about how chess should be played.

To most top players, theory is a compendium of so-called **best** lines of play. Frequently, the reason for any of these lines being good is quite murky. Evaluations can be based upon something as ephemeral as that White ended up winning the game (possibly after many mistakes for both sides).

Weaver W. Adams was the first to enunciate the **Options** principle, which is a beautiful and simple elaboration of Lasker's rule of "knights before bishops". He showed me how the moves of the chess opening can hang together to make a plan for the smooth development of the pieces. However, he made the mistake of applying these ideas to 1 e4, which is not the correct first move. Therefore, as was somewhat apparent from the beginning, his method of development did not always conform to his principles, and he even changed what he thought was the best 2nd move, later in his career.

Adams thought that after 1 e4 e5 the correct move was 2 ♗c4 (later he changed his preference to 2 ♘c3). However, neither of these moves addresses the most important problem; namely, how to challenge the centre. The correct move, if there is one, must be one of d4, f4, ♘f3, all of which attack the centre. Without this, the initiative will gradually fade, as Black is not forced to make any concessions. White must use his tempo advantage to attack, and beginning with the second move, the centre is the logical place to attack. One cannot expect to win a game of chess by just developing one's pieces. The advantage of half a tempo is not enough for that. One must use that tempo advantage to attack the centre and force further concessions. Adams's ideas were not up to that.

By 1950, study had convinced me that if there was to be a 'White to Play and Win' from the starting position, it had to start with 1 d4, not 1 e4. The reason has to do with positional principles.

The standard advantages are usually given as:
a) Material;
b) King Safety;
c) Pawn Structure;
d) Board Control;
e) Development;
f) Piece Placement;
g) Mobility.

Seldom do books do more than expound on what these advantages are. However, to play well, one must know much more than that these advantages exist. The questions that were now burning to be resolved were:

a) Which of these advantages was the most important and by how much over the next most important;

b) How did these advantages relate to each other.

Study had convinced me that **Board Control** is the most important thing to achieve right after maintaining material balance, and keeping the king safe. Board Control is **very** important in that he who controls the board can prevent his opponent's pieces from occupying good squares. So Board Control is worth fighting for. **Board Control** alone was enough to determine the best first move: 1 d4 controls three centre squares, while no other move controls more than two. It was clear that Options also had an important place along with the standard chess advantages.

When I began to play correspondence chess in 1955, I also undertook the study of exactly how the white side should be played; i.e. what **The System** is all about. Every game in which I had White began with 1 d4. Further, the slow rate of play of correspondence chess allowed me to work out in detail (not always successfully) just how each opening line should be pursued.

I was able to learn a lot about the difficult subject of how the various advantages interface, and what their relative values are. Suffice it to say, that this can depend a lot upon the position at hand. We give several illustrations of this in the following sections and throughout the book. However, one thing one can be certain of: **it is never correct to make a move that flagrantly violates one of the Principles given above.** Selecting a move will be the process of finding the move that does the most to obey all principles, without violating any one in some important way. If play has been **System** correct to this point, the next move should also obey the principles. Sometimes it is possible to find the correct move simply by process of elimination: a certain move is the only one that is both materially sound, and obeys all the principles; so it must be the correct move.

In this connection I certainly learned that one should be very careful about 'winning' a pawn in the opening as it almost always involves making some serious concession. Even to exchange one's good bishop is almost always bad. This bishop, by virtue of being the good one, is the major guardian of one colour of squares. This is because one's own pawns are on the other colour and guarding the squares of that colour. To swap it off will almost always mean that control over these less guarded squares will be weakened, and this will enable Black to get serious counterplay.

Over the years, **The System** has been instrumental in revealing lines of play that lead to permanent advantages for White against very reputable black defences. Although not all openings have yet yielded their secrets, there are enough reputable openings that have been overwhelmed by **System** moves to make one believe that the others will fall eventually. Thus, it is not unreasonable to claim that White with best play can maintain a permanent advantage, no matter what line of play Black chooses. This is no automatic win. The principles only take White through the opening; then he must play the middlegame and ending. However, the information in Chapter 1 should help greatly with that.

Examples of the Application of Certain Important Principles

Board Control

The most important principle is **Board Control**. In the opening, this means the centre and particularly the squares on White's own side of the board. What it means to **Control** a square is clearly defined in Chapter 1, p.20. The **Board Control** principle is already sufficient to choose the correct first move for White. If we consider the candidates to be 1 e4, 1 d4, 1 c4, 1 ♘f3, and 1 f4, it is easy to see that a centre pawn can control at most two of the valuable centre squares and the same is true for a knight. However, the only move that controls three central squares is 1 d4, since the queen also controls the d4-square.

For understanding **the System**, it is important to note that although 1 e4 allows White's pieces more scope, this is not the important factor, whereas centre control is. The fact that the pawn at e4 is unprotected should sooner or later cause White some problems there.

To understand why board control is important, consider Adams's original formulations for *White to Play and Win*, which he put forward in a book with that title. Adams was basically a tactician, but he longed for some order in the way the game should be played. He found that order in principles that govern how the pieces should be developed. In this kind of scheme, it would be perfectly fine for a game to start 1 e4 e5 2 ♘f3 ♘c6 3 ♘c3 ♘f6 4 ♗b5 ♗b4 5 d3 d6 6 ♗g5 *(D)*.

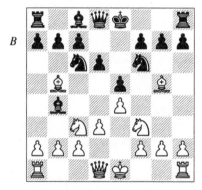

This is very systematic, but it leads to very tranquil positions where action can only be brought about by piece play. Here each side controls its own set of squares, and the conflict requires some attempt to take over the opponent's set.

Adams recognized that such play was insufficient for advantage, and wanted to get the pawns into the game also. He rightly considered the move f4 to be essential to White's plan, as this is the correct way to attack the centre; i.e. with a wing pawn. However, it was well known that 2 f4 (the King's Gambit) was unsound, so he sought for some way to prepare this. This is already a clue that he was on the wrong path. If one has to prepare an attack on the centre, then what will the opponent do with that unit of time? Certainly not sit around.

His first attempt, 2 ♗c4 did introduce some interesting tactics, but against the eminently solid and counter-attacking 2...♘f6, White can make no serious headway. In particular, 3 f4 does not work[1], so he must play either 3 ♘c3 or 3 d3, both of which are defensive in nature and give up the initiative. Ultimately, Adams switched to 2 ♘c3, but this preparatory move cannot possibly be right. It is purely defensive in nature as **it attacks no new squares in the centre**. So while Adams may have had a good scheme for developing the pieces, it failed to deal with the major problem of Board Control.

If there is a correct move after 1 e4 e5 it has to be 2 f4, since 2 ♘f3 limits further aggression in the centre because the f2-pawn will not be able to participate. Since, 2 f4 is not feasible, it is likely that 1 e4 is wrong.

A corollary to the understanding of the importance of control, is the understanding that the least valuable unit available is the best controller. This is because it is the most expendable, and thus can sell its life most dearly. Since pawns are the least valuable units, this accounts readily for Philidor's well-known dictum that "Pawns are the Soul of Chess". If at all possible, control should be exercised by pawns; certainly on the front lines of play. This leaves the pieces to support the pawns and augment their attacks. How to do this smoothly is the subject of the next section.

The Option Principle

The question of how to achieve the aims of the piece development process and get each piece to its optimum location is left to the theory of **Options**. In Chapter 1, p.29, we defined what it means to have a piece developed properly. The Option Principle assures that each white piece gets developed properly in support of the foot-soldiers: the pawns that do the primary controlling.

---

1   There are any number of tricky departures with this move, most of which I investigated as a teenager; however, if Black plays solidly they each come to nothing.

The **Option Principle** is one of the keystones of **The System**, together with **Board Control**, and should be well understood. To repeat: the **Option Principle** states **"Make the move (develop the piece) which does the least to reduce your options to make other important moves"**.

For instance, if you have a bishop that could be effectively developed to any of three different squares, and a knight which is really useful only on one particular square, then develop the knight first if it does not block any of the bishop moves. This kind of thing comes up in the position reached after the moves 1 d4 d5 2 c4 e6. Here, it is quite clear that the b1-knight belongs on c3 to continue the attack against the black d5-pawn. The c1-bishop can also move, but it is not at all clear where it should go. So, we make the indicated move 3 ♘c3, while awaiting further developments that will determine where the queen's bishop is best positioned. We also do not consider 3 e3, as it blocks the c1-bishop and commits the pawn to a one-square advance when it could possibly advance two squares some time in the future.

In Chapter 4, we will encounter some examples where the location of a bishop can be determined before the location of a knight, and how to decide such issues. Until we

get to some actual complicated examples, the reader should keep in mind that:

a) Board Control issues determine where a piece is best placed;

b) A piece or pawn may have several optimum or near-optimum placements;

c) The Option Principle decides which piece to move next and where.

The above three lines provide a concise statement of what **The System** is all about.

As a rudimentary illustration of why many moves should be rejected on **System** grounds, we can look at the position after 1 d4 d5 *(D)*.

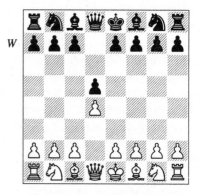

Here White could potentially choose from any of the following 'reasonable' 2nd moves, all of which have been played at some time in master practice: 2 ♘c3, 2 ♘f3, 2 e4, 2 c4, 2 e3, 2 f3, 2 ♗f4 and 2 ♗g5. Let us apply Board Control and

Options to see why certain moves fail.

a) 2 ♘c3 limits the attack on the centre by blocking the c2-pawn, which can now no longer participate immediately in the attack on d5.

b) 2 ♘f3 is a fine developing move that only blocks the f2-pawn. However, it does nothing to control new squares, and gives up the option of playing ♘ge2 and f3. The latter could help in the fight over the important e4-square. Playing ♘f3 basically yields the e4-square to Black.

c) 2 e4 would be wonderful if it were tactically sound. As it is, it just loses a pawn, that can at best be recovered with a very much inferior position.

d) 2 c4 is the correct move as it attacks the key centre d5-square with a wing pawn. The issue of whether this move loses a pawn is one that has been resolved by earlier masters. The reply 2...dxc4 does not win a pawn. Instead, Black has given up the centre at least temporarily, leaving the important e4- and c4-squares to White.

e) 2 e3 is again a passive developing move, but it blocks in the c1-bishop and gives up on any chance of a two-square advance by the e-pawn.

f) 2 f3 threatens 3 e4 and is thus a legitimate candidate to be the correct **System** move. However, it is very premature since it does not

make any direct attack. Therefore, Black can immediately counter-attack effectively with 2...c5, after which he stands better. It also blocks the potential development of the g1-knight at a time when Black has as yet made no concessions.

g) 2 ♗f4 and 2 ♗g5 both decide on the bishop location prematurely, and even more importantly do nothing toward increasing control of the centre.

Thus 2 c4 emerges as the only useful move which does not block any future options.

When is it All Right to Block a Pawn Advance?

The above discussions have brought to light an important point that we have not discussed as yet: when is it all right to block a pawn advance. Consider the position after 1 d4 d5 2 c4 e6 3 ♘c3 c5 4 cxd5 exd5 *(D)*.

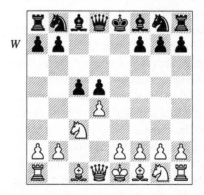

What is the correct **System** move here?

There are many types of centre positions.

a) Sometimes, Black competes in the centre, as in 1 d4 d5, and White will now aim his attack at d5;

b) Sometimes, Black chooses not to contest the centre, as in 1 d4 ♘f6 2 c4 g6 3 ♘c3 ♝g7 4 e4;

c) Sometimes, Black chooses to challenge the white centre as in 1 d4 ♘f6 2 c4 c5, when the advance 3 d5 is correct.

Here we are faced with a somewhat different situation. Black has chosen to contest the centre and created a weakness in the process. With black pawns at c5 and d5, the d5-pawn will sooner or later get weak, and possibly isolated. Since this pawn is weak, it would not be correct to attack it with a pawn. So, the move e4 is no longer of interest.

So in this situation, White must play differently. The first question to deal with is what to do about Black's threat to play 5...cxd4 6 ♕xd4 ♘c6, which would give him good piece play and drive White's queen around. There are basically three options:

a) 5 e3, which is terrible because it blocks in the c1-bishop among other things;

b) 5 dxc5, which isolates the d5-pawn but allows the advance 5...d4, whereupon Black's game becomes very active;

c) 5 ♘f3, which blocks the f2-pawn but steadies the centre against the possible 5...cxd4.

When one considers that White no longer really wants to play e4, then the loss of mobility of the f2-pawn no longer matters. Further, since the battle for the centre has become very active, White must be prepared to participate there with his pieces, so 5 ♘f3 is definitely the right move.

When the competition in the centre goes on slowly, it is frequently correct to aim to play the knight to e2 after having played ♝d3 first and then be able to challenge the e4-square with f3. However, here things are moving very fast, and White must be prepared to defend his centre. Given, that Black has already made a major weakening, White can forget about the role of the f2-pawn for now.

The f2-pawn is about the only pawn that is ever blocked in **System** play.

a) The d-pawn advances on the first move.

b) c4 follows on the second move unless Black has played 1...c5, 1...e5, or 1...♘c6, in which case it may be postponed a move or two.

c) Nothing is ever put in the way of the e-pawn.

d) The major decisions about when to play ♘f3 and block the f2-pawn are like the one above, and in situations such as after 1 d4 ♘f6 2 c4 g6 3 ♘c3 ♗g7 4 e4 d6. Here one of the popular moves is 5 ♘f3, but this blocks one of White's most effective set-ups that involves playing 5 f3. Such cavalier blockages of the f2-pawn are not to be advised. The f2-pawn is a very important actor in **System** play, and should not be shoved to the side-lines without good reason.

The Process of Selecting an Actual Move

The following procedure is based on some protocols about how grandmasters do move selection taken by de Groot (*Thought and Choice in Chess*). We have implemented the essence of the procedure in an algorithm known as the B* algorithm (*The B* Tree Search Algorithm: A Best-First Proof Procedure*, *Artificial Intelligence*, 1979). The rules below give this procedure in a form easily understood by humans. Following these rules will produce the correct **System** move.

The process of selecting a move involves some uncertainty about the value of most moves. A move has an **Optimistic** value, which is the value that will result if you get to carry out all your plans. It also has a **Realistic** value, which is the value that will result against best resistance by your opponent.

1) Qualify those moves that accord with **System** principles to be candidates for the correct move.

2) Calculate the Optimistic and Realistic values for each of these.

3) If the Realistic value of one move is no worse than the Optimistic value of any of the others, this is the best move; play it.

4) If there is some overlap between the Optimistic value of a move that does not have the best Realistic value, and the best Realistic value, then there is doubt as to which move is best. In that case, deepen the calculations.

5) Go back to step 2.

Here are some other guidelines that will stand you in good stead.

a) Don't be afraid to pursue your objectives systematically even if a pawn or two may have to be invested.

b) Artificial moves are seldom **System** moves. For instance, in the line from the Tarrasch Defence 1 d4 d5 2 c4 e6 3 ♘c3 c5 4 cxd5 cxd4 do not now play 5 ♕a4+ and follow with ♕xd4. 5 ♕xd4 is the move you want to play, and it should be played immediately without giving Black any further developing tempi.

c) It is frequently useful to give up a pawn for a gain of time. For this purpose, a gain of 3 tempi is more than enough; however, be wary of gaining a pawn either with time or significant space loss.

3 Chess Dynamics

The Notion of Chunks

In the early 1930s, a Russian psychologist did an amazing experiment. He took two groups of chess players, one strong and one weak, and showed them chess positions for a duration of two seconds. After two seconds the position was removed from view, and the player was asked to reconstruct as much of the position as he could. Master and grandmaster strength players were able to reconstruct about 90% of the position, while weaker players were able to only place about 50% or less of the pieces correctly. At first, this result could seem to stem from the fact that good chess players may have much better memory than poor players.

However, in the second part of the experiment, positions were shown that had been constructed by randomly placing pieces on the board. In this part of the experiment, the good players did not do any better than the poor ones.

What had been shown is that good chess players see some **structure** in a chess position. This structure aids in the way the position is perceived, thus allowing the better player to perceive more of the position in terms of its 'meaning' rather than as a set of individual pieces. These perceptual units were called 'chunks' by the psychologists, and we will use this term in our discussions. Chunks are found not only in chess. In fact, in simple things such as seeing a word rather than a set of letters, the chunking mechanism is quite evident. In 1938, at the AVRO tournament of 8 World Candidate chess players, De Groot, a Dutch psychologist, repeated the experiment and obtained essentially the same result (*Thought and Choice in Chess*).

The nature of the human brain is such that it can hold up to seven chunks without losing any of them due to overload. Thus, there are usually between 2 and 7 chunks present in an interpretation of the world at a certain level. This essentially assigns a 'Signature' to the situation being perceived. This signature allows for classification, and one can learn the properties of situations that have the same Signature. This allows an abstraction of the current situation that can be used to index to a higher level of understanding based upon 'chunks present'.

The interesting question for us is: "What is the meaning of these chunks for understanding chess and how to play it better?". We are all well aware of the 'king-safety' chunks which consists of a king position (usually castled) and the pawns in front of the king that shield it from attack. However, there are hundreds of thousands more chunks, as has been estimated by experiment by Herbert Simon and his co-workers (*Perception in Chess, Cognitive Psychology*, 1973). Chunks allow a good player essentially to parse, or make sense of, a chess position, as he would a sentence spoken in a natural language.

Types of Chunks

There are chunks for all sorts of advantages that a good chess player does well to recognize. To name just a few:

a) Which are the best minor pieces;

b) Cooperation of pieces;

c) Permanent fixed targets for attack;

d) What is well defended and what is not;

e) Square colour complexes.

Below, we present a few illustrations.

In the following diagram we show a position where on the left side the bishop and pawns cooperate well to control the territory in their vicinity, while on the right side the bishop

Good bishop; fair bishop

and pawns are in each other's way, thus devaluing the bishop, and causing board control problems.

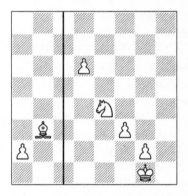

The white pieces defend each other

In the right-hand side of this diagram, we show a string of pieces that mutually defend one another, whereas on the left side is a very simple mutual defence of bishop and pawn.

Colour Complex

In this position, White is weak on the light squares while Black is weak on the dark squares

As said, the GM recognizes at least 100,000 such chunks (source: *Perception in Chess*). This is his library that allows him to interpret a position quickly and accurately. We will not be concerned with how to build up a chunk library here. It probably comes from much practice and understanding of what went on. However, the ability to have chunks and analyse positions for things that hang together functionally is an essential part of playing good chess, and we will invoke this from time to time.

How to Recognize Chunks

Chunks can deal with a square, or a facet of the position. Our notation will be:

Chunk (Facet or Square; List of Piece Squares involved)

Examples of chunks about a facet are things such as king safety, queenside development, and pawn structure.

An Attack/Defence Chunk

One of the critical things that makes pieces a part of a chunk are the attack and defence relationships among the pieces of the chunk. There is a focus of the chunk which is the piece or square of contention. The other pieces are part of the chunk as they are essential for the attack or defence. When pieces are in need of defence this is obvious, but in certain cases it is possible for a chunk to be about a square, such as a square where a piece could give mate. A simple tactical chunk is shown in the above diagram. This Chunk (e5; W: e2; B: e5, d6) has the black knight as object, the white e2-rook attacking it, the black d6-pawn defending it. These three pieces form the chunk.

There are the above described 'tactical' chunks, and there are also 'positional' chunks. We have already mentioned the king-safety chunk, and there are other positional chunks such as the position of a fianchettoed bishop in Chunk (king's fianchetto; W: g2, f2, g3, h2). Clearly, just as there are more complicated tactical chunks, so there are more complicated positional chunks. One intriguing type of positional chunk is the so-called fortress position. Here, because of certain properties, an inferior force can hold off a superior force. One simple type of fortress chunk is seen in the following diagram.

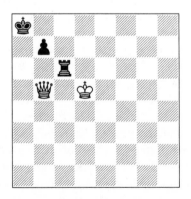

A Fortress Chunk

This position is a guaranteed draw because the rook can maintain its position by letting the black king do the moving. In this way the white king cannot penetrate near the black king, and without that the position is drawn.

It can be seen from the above discussion that chunks have some dynamics that hold them together. These dynamics could be of several types:

a) Pieces attacking and defending a square or squares (occupied or not);

b) Pieces cooperating to control a zone of the board;

c) In the case of the king only, pawns that shelter the king.

Chunks as Meaningful Entities

With experience, a player will learn to recognize chunks. That in itself is very useful, as for instance it is useful to recognize a good king-safety position from a poor one. However, this is only a tiny part of the action.

A story is told, and everything I know of indicates this is a true story, of the young Akiba Rubinstein who was a mediocre hanger-on at the chess club in Lodz, Poland. At one point, he decided to depart and was not seen or heard from for about 6 months. When he returned to the chess club, he challenged the Champion, Salwe, who was also champion of Poland, to a game. To everyone's surprise he won. Thereafter a match was arranged, and this was drawn. A new match resulted in a decisive victory for Rubinstein. He had leap-frogged from a mediocre player to one of the best players in the world. How could he have done this in such a short time?

In my analysis of the games of my predecessors, I single out the games of Rubinstein as being the first of what I call the **Dynamic School of Chess**. In the months he was absent from Lodz, Rubinstein had discovered Dynamics. This can be seen in his games, where frequently material is sacrificed for strong positional advantages, and where the pieces specialize in dazzling displays of co-operation.

Rubinstein played rook and pawn endings better than anyone at that time or before him. Rook and pawn endings are generally regarded as the most difficult, as the number of pieces on the board is small, and yet the rooks represent a lot of power. Managing this power well is the hallmark of the master player. Rubinstein was able to win rook and pawn endings by understanding things about the value of rooks occupying attacking positions so as to place the opponent's rooks on defence. For this, it was first necessary to create weak enemy pawns that could not be supported by other enemy pawns.

All this, he did with consummate artistry, winning positions that up to that time would have been considered so drawish, that they would not be worth playing. A wonderful example of his skill at this is shown below.

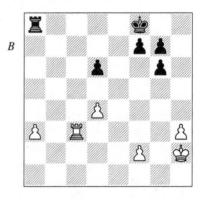

Spielmann – Rubinstein
St Petersburg 1909

In this position, material is level and Black even has a pair of doubled pawns. However, he stands much better based upon an understanding of the chunk layout. White's pawns are all isolated, and must be defended by pieces when attacked. The pawns on the kingside can be defended easily as long as the white king stays there. However, there is a chunk of two white queenside pawns that must be defended, and the black rook can attack them both, while the white rook must defend them. Thus, this chunk of 4 pieces speaks to the defensive nature of the white position. Beyond that one cannot tell much. The black king has more possibilities for infiltrating the white position than the white king has for infiltrating the black. The dynamics of these chunks become apparent as we watch the game unfold. However, one thing is clear from the play: one player understands the nature of defensive chunks and the other does not.

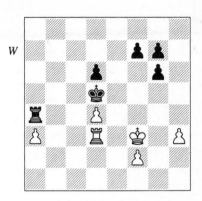

1 ...	罩a4!
2 罩d3	曾e7
3 曾g3	曾e6
4 曾f3	

White would do well to play 4 d5+! 曾e5 5 曾f3 g5 6 曾e3 曾f5 7 曾f3 f6 8 曾e3 g4 9 hxg4+ 曾xg4, when his king can head for b3 while Black advances his kingside pawns and the issue is still very much in doubt. To play 4 d5+ would be to remove one of the targets to another square which allows more room for the defence. On the other hand to allow the black king into d5 and c4 seems to be utter folly as White soon is in zugzwang and must lose a pawn. The contents of the Chunk (queenside; W: a3, d4, d3; B: a4) is now quite evident.

| 4 ... | 曾d5 (D) |
| 5 曾e2 | |

It was better to play 5 h4 so as to prevent Black's next move. Play could then continue 5...f6 6 曾e2 and White's defensive resources are much better than those he got in the game.

For the moment Black dare not continue 5...罩xd4 6 罩xd4+ 曾xd4, whereupon White's outside passed a3-pawn will be the dominant dynamic factor, and White stands much superior in a pawn ending that will be played on the kingside, while the black king is absent on the queenside.

| 5 ... | g5! |

Fixing another weakness to be attacked: the h3-pawn.

6 罩b3	f6
7 曾e3	曾c4
8 罩d3	d5! (D)

Now White is in zugzwang, and must give ground. Soon a pawn will be lost.

9 曾d2	罩a8
10 曾c2	罩a7
11 曾d2	罩e7

White is again in zugzwang, and must make an unhappy move, whereupon Black will encroach decisively.

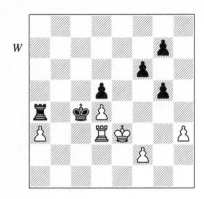

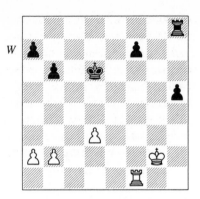

The point of the example is how to take advantage of weaknesses by attacking them, and forcing the opponent to defend them. A defending piece is worth less than an identical attacking piece. Thus, the values of pieces can shift according to their roles in a chunk. At this point White must lose a pawn. 12 ♔c2 ♖e2+ 13 ♖d2 ♖xd2+ 14 ♔xd2 ♔b3! 15 ♔e3 ♔xa3 16 ♔f3 ♔b3 17 ♔g4 ♔c4 leads to an easy win for Black. After Black has won the pawn, the rest is a matter of shepherding the advantage to a win.

Another example of dynamic decision-making in a rook ending is my game against Estrin in the 5th World Correspondence Championship. Here Black is a pawn ahead, but it is difficult to utilize it. Black's f7-pawn is attacked, and he must decide what to do. If he defends it with ...♖h7, planning to advance the h-pawn, he ruins the dynamics of his

Estrin – Berliner
*5th World Correspondence Ch
Final, 1965-8*

position, as the h-pawn will not get very far, and in the meantime White will attack and exchange the pawns on the queenside, leaving a drawn position. For Black to play ...♔e6 to defend his f7-pawn is useless as the king will be harassed by checks starting with ♖e1+. Black must recognize that his assets consist of passed outside pawns on the kingside, and the fact that the white d3-pawn is only a fixture since it can assume no meaningful role, and will be captured at Black's convenience.

With this understanding, it is clear that in order for Black to win, he must play on the queenside against the seemingly secure pawns there. One should also understand that if play is to be concentrated on the queenside, then the black f- & h-pawns are the outside passed pawns, and only one of them is enough to distract the white king (preferably the h-pawn). With this in mind, the winning plan becomes clear. Black will sacrifice his f7-pawn in order to threaten the white queenside pawns with his rook, thus requiring the white rook to stand guard. Then, he will march his king to the queenside via the centre, gobbling up the d-pawn in the process. Meanwhile, White can only send his king to capture the h-pawn. The game continued:

| 31 ... | ♖c8! |
| 32 ♖xf7 | ♖c7! |

White dare not now exchange, as the pawn ending is an easy win.

| 33 ♖f2 | ♔e5! (D) |

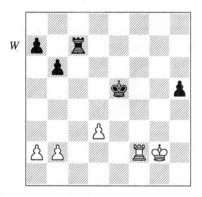

34 a4?

An awful move that voluntarily weakens the queenside, which is just what Black wants to accomplish. White is lost anyway, as is shown by 34 ♔g3! ♔d4 35 ♔h4 ♔xd3 36 ♔xh5 ♖c2! (D) and now:

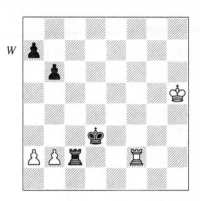

a) 37 ♖f3+ ♔d2! and then:

a1) 38 b4 ♖c3! 39 ♖f2+ ♔e1! 40 ♖h2 ♖a3! 41 ♔g5 ♖a4 42 ♖b2 ♔d1 and wins.

a2) 38 b3! ♔c1! 39 a4 ♖b2! 40 a5 (otherwise Black plays ...a5) 40...b5 41 a6 b4 42 ♔g4 ♔c2 43 ♖f7 ♖xb3 44 ♖xa7 ♖a3 45 ♖b7 b3 46 a7 b2 and wins.

a3) 38 ♖a3 a5 39 ♖b3 ♖c5+ 40 ♔g4 b5 41 ♔f4 ♔c2 42 ♔e4 ♔b1 43 ♔d4 ♖h5 44 ♖a3 a4! 45 ♔c3 ♖h4! wins.

b) 37 ♖f7 ♖c5+ 38 ♔g4 ♖a5 39 ♖f3+! ♔d2!! 40 a3 (40 b3 ♖a3!) 40...♔c2 41 ♖f2+ ♔b3 42 ♔f4 ♖b5! 43 ♔e4 ♔a2! 44 ♖f7 a6! 45 ♖a7 ♖a5! 46 ♖b7 b5 and wins.

The dynamics of attack and defence of the pawns is very intricate, involving changes of venue by the black rook from side attack to frontal and rear, by means of checks, and the infiltration of the black king to either attack the pawns or cramp the white rook.

34	...	♔d4
35	a5	♔xd3
36	♖f3+	♔c2 *(D)*

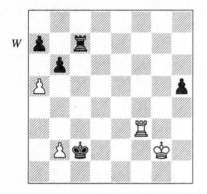

No matter how White plays, his pawns are very weak and easily attacked and won.

37	b4	b5!
38	a6	♖c4
39	♖f7	♖xb4
40	♖h7	♖g4+
41	♔f3	b4
42	♖xa7	b3
	0-1	

The Interaction of Chunks

Now, we come to the difficult part: why do chess-players recognize chunks; what good are they? It is nice to be able to tell a good king-safety from a poor one, but isn't there much more to this? Yes, there is and with the exception of calculating correctly in tactics, this is the most important part of playing good chess. **The correct understanding of chunk interaction leads directly to strategies.**

In science and mathematics there is something called an abstraction space. An abstraction space deals with future possibilities. In chess, this is not the space of moves that are possible now which would form the basis for tactical calculation. Rather it is the space of locations that any and all the pieces and pawns could occupy in the future. This is the space of strategic planning. If you can visualize such realistic future possibilities, you will be able to reason about future positions that can be encountered. So we conclude that:

1) Chunks are entities that point the way for proceeding strategically.

2) Chunks can interact with other chunks to change the evaluation that would apply if only one of them were present.

2a) If one side has poor king safety it is usually a good idea to swap pieces in order to lessen the likelihood of a successful attack. However, if that side also has serious pawn-structure weaknesses, then swapping pieces could lead to a clearly losing ending. So, both chunks influence the decision.

2b) If one has fair king safety, one can undertake action on the other side of the board only with great caution. However, if the centre is blocked, then one can do so with a feeling of relative security. This is because any attack must come from the front or the side (rather unlikely), as the opponent's forces will not be able to come diagonally through the centre.

3) There are many strategies governing attack:

3a) When the opponent's king safety is poor;

3b) When ahead in development;

3c) When having a weak pawn structure.

4) If you have many important pawns on the same colour as one of your bishops, that bishop will be less useful. A less useful bishop is frequently worth less than the average knight. This is one of the things that makes having the two bishops so useful; one can usually exchange the worse of the pair for a knight.

5) If you have a remote (from the king) pawn majority, it is advantageous to swap pieces, as this will make it easier to advance the majority.

The possibilities are nearly endless. Such high-level judgements can be made about any pair of chunks. As previously mentioned, there are 2 to 7 chunks in a position. Each chunk could affect the appraisal of another chunk, so there may be as many as 21 ($7 \times 6 / 2$) simple chunk interactions. It is also possible for a chunk's value to be influenced by two or more other chunks. These chunk interactions define what the position is about and the nature of the correct strategy for each side. This is a very difficult subject, and one can find examples daily in grandmaster practice where wrong decisions are made because of a lack of understanding of the dictates of the correct strategy. One such example is given in the following diagram.

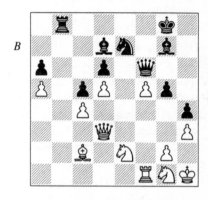

Korchnoi – Hort
Palma de Mallorca 1969
Black to play
What is the correct 'view'?

This position can be seen as a middlegame in which White is attacking the black king behind the advanced f5-pawn. This will almost certainly succeed in time, as White's pieces are all poised for this attack, and Black's king safety has already been weakened by the advance of all his pawns in front of the king.

However, if a wholesale exchange took place on f5, in which Black gave up queen and two pieces for queen, rook and pawn, we would have an ending. With the correct chunk-interaction view of this ending, one could see that White's pieces are massed on the kingside, now without any clear duty to perform, while White has two weak pawns on the queenside, one of which must certainly fall to the invasion of the black rook. After that, the material balance would be ♖ + ♙ vs ♗ + ♘, which is nearly equal. Further, the black rook and bishop and newly passed pawn would be a formidable force on the queenside, and would cause White many problems. The two white knights are too far away to stop the advance of the pawn in an effective way.

Seen in this way, it is clear that such endings are very much in Black's favour, so he should recover his pawn by 1...♗xf5! 2 ♖xf5 ♕xf5 3 ♕xf5 ♘xf5 4 ♗xf5 ♖b4! 5 ♗c8! ♖xc4 6 ♗xa6 ♖a4 and Black has a clear advantage.

Instead Black played 1...♖f8? 2 g4 hxg3 3 ♘xg3 ♕d4 4 ♘1e2 and eventually lost. He had made the mistake of analysing variations instead of **chunks**. The chunk analysis would have clearly revealed that White is in a great deal of trouble on the queenside after the exchanges on f5.

There are also strategies that are intended solely to increase or decrease the advantage within a chunk. One such example is luring pawns of your opponent onto the colour of his bishop that is already partially bad. In the next section, we present an example that shows how on an open board, a bishop still can be really bad.

The Analysis of Chunk Interaction

Chunking Clarifies the Position

Can White win?

In this position White is two healthy pawns ahead. If White had any other minor piece except the dark-squared bishop, Black could safely resign. Even if the d-pawn were on d5 rather than d6, Black could only offer token resistance. However, here the bishop and its own pawns interact badly, and the question is whether White can win despite this handicap. Here are the chunks:

a) Chunk (centre pawns; W: d6, e5, f6, d5; B: d7, e6): White has two connected passed pawns, but it is not clear if they can advance.

b) Chunk (g-file pawns; W: g4, d5, f6; B: g6, e6): the question is whether the g6-pawn can be effectively attacked by the white king.

There are two potential plans for White to win:

a) Try to advance the centre pawns, in particular the e5-pawn. This fails because the e6-knight has potentially eight squares to move to and they cannot all be covered by the bishop, pawns and king. So the king just stays put on d7, and the knight just moves back and forth and the pawns cannot advance.

b) Try to infiltrate with his king through g5 in order to win the g6-pawn. This involves the white king going to h4, from where it could infiltrate. The knight is the only guardian of the g5-square, so it must stay put. However, in that situation, the black king has been freed, and can just move back and forth.

So White has no chance of winning this position. I do not think there is a computer in the world that would realize that this position is a draw. As of now, no highly rated computer chunks!

A Complicated Example with Values

The following position is from the Berliner Variation of the Fritz Two Knights. It occurs after the moves 1 e4 e5 2 ♘f3 ♘c6 3 ♗c4 ♘f6 4 ♘g5 d5 5 exd5 b5 6 ♗f1 ♘d4 7 c3 ♘xd5 8 ♘e4 ♕h4 9 ♘g3 ♗g4 10 f3 e4! 11 cxd4 ♗d6 (D).

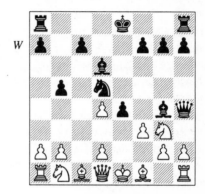

**The Berliner
Two Knights Position**

We now analyse the chunks and assign values to them. The value is the increment that should be added (subtracted) beyond what one would get if one merely totals up the material in the chunk. A '+' value is something in White's favour, and a '−' is something in Black's. By looking at the board in chunks, we can determine excess values and deficient values. We can start by thinking of the value of the chunk as the value of the pieces in it. The fact that a piece can be in more than one chunk is of no concern. We are interested only in how that piece's participation in the chunk changes the value of the chunk. One piece can participate in more than one chunk, and affect the value of each. For instance, a white bishop can be participating in two chunks. One chunk has a value of +0.5 which is good for White, and the other has a value of −1.2, which is good for Black. Removing the white bishop from the board (by exchange) may change the value of both, one, or neither chunk, but it is a decision that must be made consciously, with the chunk structure in mind. Also, we must bear in mind that all that is being evaluated is the value of the **interaction** of the pieces. Whether a piece is *en prise* or not does not matter, as the effect of this will be determined by tactics. However, the positional and strategic consequences are what the value of the chunk is all about.

An Initial Evaluation of Chunks
An enumeration of the chunks in the previous diagram reveals the following. After describing each chunk, we discuss the factors that may affect its value, and then give an estimate of its actual value. We use a scale in which a pawn is worth one, and plus values are good for White, and minus values good for Black. Thus, if a chunk has a value of +0.5 it is worth approximately half a pawn for White. The idea of presenting chunk values is to give the reader an idea of how much is at stake in certain chunks. No one can estimate chunk values with perfect accuracy (even a knight is not always worth the same amount). This is especially true in a position that is in such a state of high flux as the one that is about to be presented. Chunk values are approximate, but what is very important is how the value shifts up or down as the result of actions on the board. In the given position, White is ahead by a knight and this is +3.2 units.

We now examine how the chunks represent additional value for each player, and how this compensates for material.

1) Chunk (g3; W: h2, g3; B: h4, d6): the black queen and black bishop attack, and only the h2-pawn defends the white knight. Value depends upon whose move it is: if White −0.2; if Black −1.2.

2) Chunk (f3; W: f3, g2, d1; B: e4, g4): Black is attacking with bishop and pawn, and White is defending with queen and pawn. Value: if Black to move −0.3 as he could seriously compromise the white position with ...exf3; if White to move 0.0.

3) Chunk (White's queenside; W: a1, b1, c1, d1): White's queenside is totally undeveloped. Even if

the b1-knight were to get out, the c1-bishop will still be trapped for some time to come because the d2- and b2-pawns have not moved yet. Because of this, the a1-rook is also trapped. Value: with White to move −1.75; with Black to move −2.5. This may seem like a large value for someone not familiar with judging such advantages, but this value has been shown to be approximately correct in my computer chess implementation.

4) Chunk (White's kingside; W: f1, h1): White's kingside is also undeveloped, but not so seriously, as he can play ♗xb5+ and then 0-0. Value: −0.35.

5) Chunk (Black's development): Black has all his pieces in play except the two rooks, which are not too far away from being developed. Black's development count is −3 (two rooks and king) and White's is −7 (all pieces on back rank). This 4 unit difference translates into a value of −0.8.

6) Chunk (White's king safety): rather insecure. The value is conditioned on the amount of material remaining on the board. Value: −0.35.

7) Chunk (Black's king safety): Black's king is also in the centre. Value: +0.35.

It is very difficult to assess the value of this position accurately. The value of −3.10 (−0.2, 0.0, −1.75, −0.35, −0.8, −0.35, and +0.35) that is obtained by adding the above chunk values is approximately correct. However, there are a number of chunks that are affected by whose turn it is to move. Clearly, although White is to move, he can hardly hope to remedy his deficits in all the chunks where he is at risk. Thus, this chunk analysis supports the idea that Black may have a piece's worth of compensation for his knight minus.

When I played 10...e4! in the original game of this variation in Estrin-Berliner, 5th World Correspondence Ch 1965-8, I judged the possibilities very good for Black. Detailed analysis of the plethora of variations revealed that Black was indeed never worse than even[1]. Thus, Black has full compensation for his material inferiority due to White's lack of development and his less secure king position.

In the Estrin game and other games that I knew of, 12 ♗xb5+ ♔d8 13 0-0 was always played. In June 1997, I was made aware of a new move for White in this position: 12 ♕e2 (D), which is attributed to the American amateur Walter Muir.

---

1   The full analysis of this variation can be found in the author's *From The Deathbed of 4. ♘g5 in the Two Knight's Defence*.

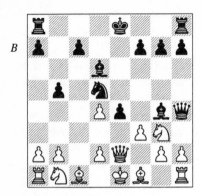

This move initially makes a bad impression as it further blocks the white kingside, but it does have some good features:

a) It pins the e4-pawn and thus neutralizes the Chunk (f3).

b) It threatens ♕xb5+, winning the d5-knight when appropriate. This latter idea is important as if Black were now to play 12...♗xg3+, 13 hxg3! ♕xh1 14 ♕xb5+ wins easily.

c) It provides a place for the white king at d1, where it is relatively secure for the next two or three moves.

Chunks Re-evaluated as the Function of the Next Move

Our method of explaining chunks will involve re-examining chunk values after some critical move or series of moves. After 12 ♕e2, things have changed a great deal, and we must now redo our chunk analysis.

1) Chunk (g3) is now worth −1.2 (because it is Black to play).

2) Chunk (f3) is now worth 0.0 because the e4-pawn is pinned.

3) Chunk (White's queenside) is now worth −2.5 (because it is Black to play).

4) Chunk (White's kingside) is now much worse since on e2 the queen blocks in the f1-bishop. Its value is now −2.0.

5) Chunk (development) still favours Black by −0.8.

6) Chunk (White's king safety) is now more in Black's favour as the white king will not be able to castle for some time to come; value = −1.5.

However, White threatens two black pieces and this affects the realization of the values, since certain steps may have to be taken to safeguard material. That is what tactics is about. Again it would be foolish to believe one can just add these numbers up.

However, it is very important to notice *all* of the above changes, as they form the backbone for deciding the correct next move for Black. And it is this decision that will decide the value of this variation. Someone looking at the position superficially may decide that now is an ideal time for Black to bring his king into safety with 12...0-0, and indeed this move was played in all games that were to be found in the database to end 1997.

Based on the chunk values presented, one could ask "Is this the appropriate thing to do?" By this move Black only gets rid of a +0.35 inferiority, as the black king is in no great danger in the centre, so the only point of ...0-0 is to counter the threat of ♕xb5+.

What will happen after 12...0-0 is 13 fxg4 ♗xg3+ 14 ♔d1. White's king safety has indeed been worsened, but the two valuable chunks g3 and f3 are gone, leaving Black with little activity. Further, the black light-squared bishop has been captured, and White can now play ♘c3, and ♔c2 where the king will be perfectly safe. Further, after 14...♘f6 15 ♘c3 there is a threat of ♘xe4 after which the g3-bishop will be driven away, and it has neither a good retreat nor any useful function to fulfil in any chunk.

The latter is tremendously important, and anyone not understanding the above should re-read it. The g3-bishop is essentially functionless, while Black's light-squared bishop has been captured, thus making the white king's haven at c2 secure. Noticing the changes in the chunk structure brought on by 12 ♕e2 is something that cannot be over-emphasized. By playing 12 ♕e2 White makes his kingside still more undeveloped, and essentially commits his king to staying in the centre a long time. It is well known that a king in the centre without adequate pawn shelter when there are still

many pieces on the board is in great danger, and it is not unusual for this to be worth a piece.

Let us look at the effect on the chunks after the moves 12...0-0 13 fxg4 ♗xg3+ 14 ♔d1 (D).

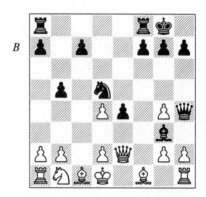

a) Chunk (f3) has disappeared; Black's g4-bishop is gone. Value lost = 0.3.

b) Chunk (g3) has been liquidated and replaced by a black g3-bishop that no longer fulfils any useful function and is exposed to attack. Value lost = 1.2.

c) Chunk (Black's king safety): Black's king gets to safety. Value gained = 0.35.

When looked at in this way, it is clear that Black got much the worse of the bargain, losing more than a pawn's worth of positional value. The g4-bishop must be saved, and the chunks on f3 and g3 maintained. The only sensible move is 12...♗e6, which indirectly protects against the threat of ♕xb5+ since the d5-knight is now protected so ♕xb5+ is met by ...♔d8.

It appears that 12...♗e6 allows White too much in the centre by 13 fxe4 (other moves are of no help to White). However, this is not the case. Black can play 13...♘b4 which forces 14 ♘a3, and then 14...0-0-0! *(D)*, which gets the king out of the centre into a less safe area, but activates the a8-rook very economically.

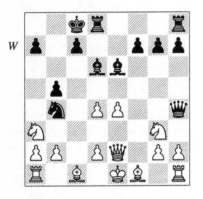

Now we can again assess the chunk structure. Black has sacrificed another pawn, making the material balance +4.2 units.

However:

1) Chunk (White's kingside) is very undeveloped: Value = −2.0.

2) Chunk (White's queenside) is very undeveloped: Value = −2.5.

3) Chunk (g3) is still active: Value = −0.2

4) Chunk (White's king safety): the white king is in the centre with not much shelter nor an easy way to castle. Value = −2.0.

5) Chunk (development) Black's development count is −1, while White's is −6. It is a huge advantage to be far ahead in development. Value = −2.0.

6) Chunk (the centre): White owns the centre, but it is quite shaky: Value = +0.5.

Although there is some duplication in the values for development and king safety, Black has tremendous positional compensation for his material inferiority. It is White's move, and he must play 15 e5!, which attacks the d6-bishop and removes all threats against g3. However, it exposes the weakness of the white centre and the king that it shelters. Black must now continue 15...♕xd4!! *(D)*.

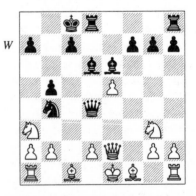

That I understood all this within one hour of having seen the Muir move 12 ♕e2 for the first time speaks well of the method being explained here. The line above *must* be correct for Black. It does the right thing to preserve the chunk advantages that Black has, without letting White off the hook. Just what the final justification of this play is and how Black accomplishes it can be found in my monograph on the Two Knights Defence (*From the Deathbed of 4. ♘g5 in the Two Knight's Defence*). Here it is important merely to follow the reasoning. The most important point is that what appears to be an exchange of pieces with 12...0-0 (the g4-bishop for the g3-knight) thus getting the black king to safety is in fact the committing of suicide. All of Black's advantages disappear for the sake of getting a king that is not really in danger into safety.

He who understands the above discussion has accomplished a lot in chess. There are two fundamental ideas that cover selection of moves under the **System** regimen:

1) **Board Control**, which is the most important, and describes how to select the pawn structure.

2) **Cooperation of the Pieces**, which includes:

2a) Chunk analysis;

2b) The idea of **Options** and how to develop the pieces to their best squares in the most economical way while helping the pawns in their quest to control the board;

2c) Notions of the weakness of pawns and how to take advantage of them.

Dynamics sets some limits on board control, lest the time consumed be too great and allow the opponent too much in the way of tactical compensation.

One Final Word on Chunking

The analysis of chunks is a vastly differing enterprise from the analysis of tactics. Chunking leads to strategic decisions. If a position already has 'character' or is about to have, one must analyse the content of the various chunks and their interaction. This is the only way to find where good is, and how to achieve it. Clearly, the status of any chunk is still governed by tactical feasibility, but just learning to think **chunks**, no matter what level your tactical skill, will improve your play.

4 The System at Work on an Actual Opening

Up to now, as you have been reading Chapter 1 on the Basic Advantages, Chapter 2 on **The System** principles, and Chapter 3 on Chess Dynamics, you may have felt that the things being said were new, reasonable or possibly not reasonable. Depending upon your playing strength and experience, you may have felt that you were being ushered into a brand new world or maybe being fibbed to. I can assure you, it is not the latter. New things always seem to be alien and demanding of suspicion. That is normal. The proof of the pudding is in the eating, and in this chapter, we will begin the eating process.

I can remember one sunny December afternoon in the 1960s during one of the US Invitational Championships in which both champion Robert J. Fischer and I were playing. Somehow, we found ourselves walking down one of Manhattan's Avenues, and of course, we were talking chess. I said to Bobby "Why don't you ever play 1 d4? It is much superior to 1 e4." He replied "How can you say that? Give me some proof." So I replied "Well, we

all think of the Slav Defence as being quite reputable. I am very close to busting it completely." "Give me some variations" was the reply.

So I told him some lines, and we discussed them as we walked down the street. He was not easy to convince, so I switched to discussing the **System** principles. I told Bobby how one goes about selecting a move in the **System**. I explained the Options principle to him, and gave some examples of how to apply it. I told him that at one time when I was not yet sure that 1 d4 was correct, I tried to apply the Option principle to the position after 1 e4 e5 to see whether 2 ♘f3 or 2 f4 was correct. At that he laughed, saying something about the fact that we all know the King's Gambit is not sound. So I agreed, and told him that was part of the reason I became convinced that 1 e4 was incorrect; because the **System** move after 1 e4 e5 is 2 f4.

Then I went into how after 1 d4 d5 it is clear that 2 c4 is best. And also after 1 d4 ♘f6, 2 c4 must be best. The only other reasonable move, 2 ♘f3, blocks the f-pawn too early on, and also allows an unfavourable transposition by 2...d5 into a line where now 3 c4 has lost much of its power because of the inability to answer 3...dxc4 by 4 e4, among other things.

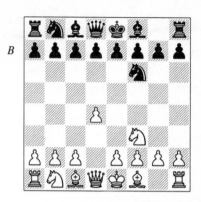

Since c4 must be played in any case, and 2 ♘f3 limits White's future options, 2 c4 must be the right way to continue. Vague notions such as fear of the Budapest Defence (1 d4 ♘f6 2 c4 e5) are just not acceptable. 2 c4 is the only way to play for an advantage, and it must be played sooner or later, so it should be played now.

Bobby said that he understood what I was saying, but in the absence of clear variations, he was not much persuaded. I found him difficult to persuade of anything, so we moved on to something else. However, the above story would be completely meaningless if it were not for one very interesting thing. Some months later, Bobby began annotating other GMs' games for *Chess Life*. He annotated a game between (I believe) Keres and Averbakh, which began 1 d4 ♘f6 2 ♘f3 *(D)*.

To my amazement I read his note which said that this move could not possibly be best!!? Wow!! He had learned something from our discussion after all. In the next issue of *Chess Life* a number of Soviet GMs took issue with Bobby's statement, saying he was arrogant to say something like that, and that 2 ♘f3 was just as good as any other move such as 2 c4. So – they still had the veil over their eyes, while Bobby had this glimpse of Nirvana.

Bobby never did anything with this knowledge. I guess the Option principle was new to him, and he never found a role for it in his variations, which were based almost exclusively on precise calculation in highly tactical situations. However, Bobby did see the logic, and clearly it made an impression on him.

So, dear reader, now off we go to see what kind of impression we shall make on you.

Applying System Principles from the Start

The first question that should naturally be asked of a system that purports to tell you how to play perfectly is "What is the best move in the starting position?". We have already alluded to this in earlier sections, but let me go through the logic once more. Let us see which **System** principles apply here. In Chapter 2, the **System** principles are given in order of importance.

These are:

1) *Tactics.* There are no tactics here.

2) *Piece Location.* There are several moves that do something to improve a piece's location, e.g. ♘f3, ♘c3, d4, and e4.

3) *Development.* Each of the above moves is also a developing move, and so would be e3, and d3.

4) *Board Control.* The only move that controls 3 squares is 1 d4. No other move controls more than 2 squares. So 1 d4 must be the right move.

Now Black has his choice of two meaningful replies: 1...d5, or 1...♘f6. In the case of 1...d5, we continue the attack on the centre from the wing by 2 c4. This is well accepted in modern theory and should not require much justification. However, what is the right move after 1...♘f6 *(D)*, which presents no targets?

This brings us to the very position in which Bobby rankled the Soviet hegemony. Let us see why he felt impelled to do that. After 1 d4 ♘f6 Black has taken no position in the centre, but only developed a piece to control some important central squares. So White has no target. How should he proceed?

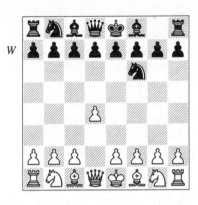

This question is solved by applying two basic **System** principles. There are the following moves that have been played in this position: 2 c4, 2 ♘f3, 2 g3, 2 e3, 2 ♘c3, and even 2 ♗g5. I am sure there are many GMs who would say that which move is preferred is a matter of style, and that the first two choices are near equal. However, **The System** disagrees. All the moves enumerated earlier, except 2 c4, have something wrong with them:

a) 2 ♘f3 blocks the f-pawn, which at this stage could possibly have some meaningful role in controlling e4. It also could lead to the following variation: 2 ♘f3 d5 3 c4 e6, and now we are in a position in which the white knight is at f3 and the b1-knight not developed, thus violating the **transposition** rule. Instead, it should be the other way around: the b1-knight should be at c3 and the other not developed. "Small matter" I can hear some players say, "I intended to continue with 4 ♘f3 (♘c3) in any case". If that is your outlook, then you are in for some education. 2 ♘f3, when played at this early stage, gives up all attempts to control e4, and violates one of the basic principles of **System** play. It also fails to attack anything. It is a move that cedes the initiative; it is wrong!

b) 2 g3 is a perfectly fine move. However, it is not a **System** move. It prematurely commits the bishop to the long diagonal when its future role is not at all clear. It gives up any hope of achieving a lasting advantage by force.

c) 2 e3 is also easy to refute logically. It commits the pawn to a one-square advance when it would really like to move up two, and blocks the c1-bishop for some time to come.

d) 2 ♘c3 seems to be logical, but after 2...d5 we have a position in which it is mandatory to attack the centre with the 3 c4 lever, and this is now not possible. So 2 ♘c3 blocks the essential lever option c4. White could now continue his idea of e4 by playing 3 f3. This move can be met by 3...♗f5, and the further 4 ♗g5 by 4...♘bd7. This is an appealing-looking way of playing; very thematic. There is only one thing wrong. It does not lead to any advantage for White. The problem turns out to be that the white c2-pawn will not participate in the attack on the centre,

and this in turn leaves White with not enough space on the queenside to be able to mobilize his forces.

e) 2 ♗g5 is an early commitment of this piece to a post that it may not belong on. There is no pin, and Black can conveniently reply 2...♘e4 and usher in complications not at all bad for him.

So why is 2 c4 correct? The answer comes, as usual, by applying **System** logic. If we play any move other than 2 c4 (except 2 e4), and Black then plays 2...d5, we will not be in position to continue the systematic attack on the centre. 2 e4 does not work because of 2...♘xe4. And 2 ♘f3 d5 3 c4 dxc4 no longer allows White to play the systematic 4 e4. So 2 c4 *(D)* **must** be correct.

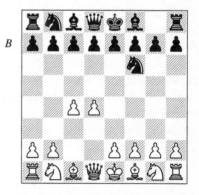

Now Black has several moves at his disposal, but for explanatory purposes I want to select 2...e6 as the move to examine. Other black second moves will be treated in later chapters. In this position, there are again several popular moves. Many people fear the Nimzo-Indian Defence (3 ♘c3 ♝b4) and therefore play 3 ♘f3. However, after 3 ♘f3, Black can reply 3...d5 and get into a variation of the QGD that is not a **System** variation.

A Small Digression

Somewhere in this book, we are going to fight a certain philosophical fight, and maybe this is the place to fight it. You have every right to say "Well, just because it is not a **System** position, why should I avoid it?" Yes, you have the right to say that, and you have the right to take from this book what you want to learn and leave the rest. I have been playing lines that I thought were **System** lines since I was 20 and I have lost some games because of this, when I made a wrong interpretation of what the **System** dictates were. However, I have always learned from those losses, and that has made **The System** better, and made this book possible. In the process, I have also become a stronger player.

You have the right to pick and choose; however, please try to understand what I present. It is not some will-of-the-wisp. It is the result of almost 50 years' worth of play and study and simulation on computers. **The System** is not a complete scientific theory, but it is very close to it, and if you want to feel you are pushing your opponent from the first move on, you would do well to consider it seriously.

To those of you who have had no doubts, and have entered upon this with an open mind, I apologize for the above digression. It was something that had to be said to those who have doubts.

What is the Correct 4th Move?

So after 3 ♘c3 Black has the choice between 3...d5 and 3...♝b4. Without going into the merits of either move, I am going to continue with 3...d5 *(D)* as allowing the best exposition of **System** principles.

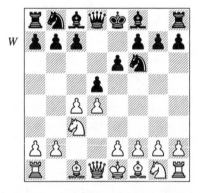

One should note here that had White played 3 ♘f3, Black would have had the option of four moves (3...b6, 3...♝b4+, 3...c5, and 3...d5) all of which appear to yield reasonable positions. Here, he has only two options (3...d5 or 3...♗b4), as he must stop White's e4 on the next move.

Now, we come to a very important point of departure. It is interesting to note that 100 years ago this position was still very new. Harry Nelson Pillsbury, that great American native genius, played 4 ♗g5 here in his games at Hastings 1895 (see *The Hastings 1895 Tournament*). He was roundly criticized by several of his fellow grandmasters for not playing the 'normal' 4 ♗f4. With only a few exceptions, the masters of that time understood very little about openings. Nowadays, no one plays 4 ♗f4 as it is recognized that it allows Black too much counterplay in the centre with an eventual ...c5. The point of 4 ♗g5 is to put pressure on the black centre as White is now threatening 5 cxd5 exd5 6 ♗xf6, when Black must reply 6...gxf6, wrecking his pawn structure, if he wishes not to lose his d-pawn. Thus, Black has no time for counterplay as he must attend to his centre first. Pillsbury recognized that, but many of his fellow GMs did not.

It is certainly logical that the bishop go to g5, and for many years I thought that was the right move. However, what 4 ♗g5 does is to put pressure on the d5-pawn while **the pawn is still mobile**. So 4 ♗g5 is the right idea, but maybe at the wrong time. Consider what would happen

after 4 ♗g5 ♗e7. Then White will again be faced with the problem of how to continue. Should he play 5 ♘f3, 5 e3 or 5 cxd5? If he plays 5 ♘f3 or 5 e3 then he has given up the fight for e4, and the books are full of lines that allow Black to fully equalize by move 12 or so. If he plays the more thematic 5 cxd5, which realizes the trade of a wing pawn for a centre pawn, then Black is no longer obliged to play ...exd5, but could reply 5...♘xd5, after which two sets of minor pieces will be traded, and the simplification helps Black's search for equality. Here White must play 6 ♗xe7 ♕xe7, and now 7 e4 ♘xc3 8 bxc3 *(D)* leaves a position that is very simplified, in which it will be hard for White to get any advantage.

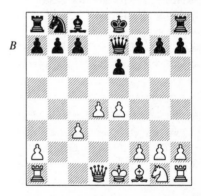

So White's search for an advantage has run aground. After 4 ♗g5 ♗e7, he must make a move that concedes e4 or allow the swap of two pairs of minor pieces.

So where did the problem arise? Clearly, in 4 ♗g5. What must be done first is to obey the **resolution** principle and resolve the central tension before it bounces back on you. So, having wrung the concession ...♘f6 out of Black, now is the time to play 4 cxd5. Why is this correct at this time? On the one hand, after 4...exd5 White has achieved his objective of a centre majority of pawns, and a fixed target at d5 to attack. Now, he can proceed with 5 ♗g5 in full control of his destiny. On the other hand, if Black chooses to play 4...♘xd5, White can continue 5 e4 ♘xc3 6 bxc3, and he has a wonderful position that is discussed in detail in Chapter 6, p.108.

Perfect System Play does not allow a Breakout

Let us follow our example with the sequence 4 cxd5 exd5 5 ♗g5 (D).

Here Black can play any number of moves that defend his centre against the threat of 6 ♗xf6, when Black has no convenient recapture. There are 5...c6, 5...♗e7, and 5...♘bd7. In case you are not familiar with the latter trap, let me point out that 5...♘bd7 gives nothing away since 6 ♘xd5?? ♘xd5! 7 ♗xd8 ♗b4+ wins easily.

However, the move 5...c6 requires some examination. One of the ideas here is possibly to deploy the c8-bishop now that the obstruction on e6 has been removed, and before White prevents it for good with ♗d3. If ...♗f5 were good for Black then White's previous moves have to be questioned. In fact, if White played anything other than 6 e3, then it would be a long time before ♗d3 could be played, and Black's ...♗f5 would become very much a reality.

So let us continue with Black playing 5...c6 (D); a move that is played sooner or later anyway.

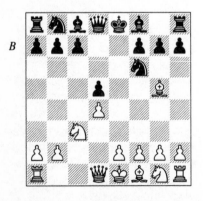

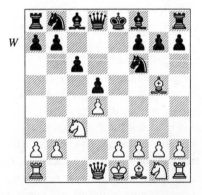

6 e3 is the normal and natural move now that the two-square advance of the e-pawn is no longer possible (at this point any attempt starting with f3 would leave the e-pawn backward, and very unlikely to advance two squares on the open e-file). We still want to control e4, however, so we do not play 6 ♘f3, as the g1-knight may be much better placed at e2, and we want to reserve the option.

Now, what would happen if Black decides to spring from his crouch by developing the c8-bishop. Let us say that after 6 e3 Black tries 6...h6 7 ♗h4 (naturally, the bishop must maintain the pin) 7...♗f5 (D).

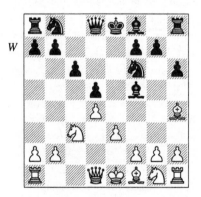

If he can get away with this, then he has equalized. However, now comes a wonderful tactical refutation of this idea. White plays 8 ♕f3!, and Black must decide what to do about his bishop and what the future of his kingside pawn structure is

going to be. I played a CC game against the French CC Champion Bergraser that continued like this:

8	♕f3!	♕d7?
9	♗xf6	gxf6
10	♘ge2	h5
11	♘g3	♗g4
12	♕xf6	♖h6
13	♕e5+!	♖e6 (D)

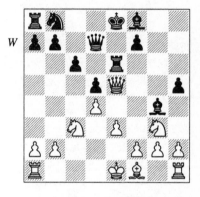

14	♘xh5!	♕e7
15	♘g7+	♗xg7
16	♕xg7	♕h4
17	♕g8+	1-0

After 17...♔e7 18 g3 ♕h5 19 h3! ♗f3 20 ♗e2 Black loses more material.

Black did not play well here, but it is a very convincing demonstration that Black dare not try to break out. Black probably must acquiesce to a very bad pawn structure, with no hope of anything except passive resistance, by playing 8...♗g6 9 ♗xf6 ♕xf6 10 ♕xf6 gxf6 11 ♘ge2 with a

wonderful endgame for White. Another bygone tactical attempt to sal-
vage the situation was this line
advocated by Pachman:

8   ...   ♛b6?! *(D)*

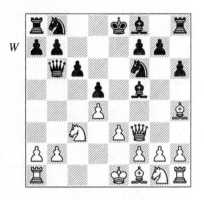

9	♛xf5!	♛xb2
10	♛c8+!	♚e7
11	♜b1!	♛xc3+
12	♚d1	g5
13	♝g3	♞e4
14	♞f3 *(D)*	

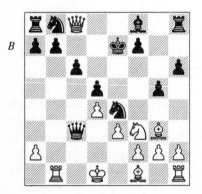

14   ...   ♝g7

15	♜xb7+	♚f6
16	♝e5+	♚g6
17	♞h4+	

...and wins.

There are side-lines such as
14...♞d7 15 ♛xa8 g4 16 ♛xb7 gxf3
17 ♛b2 fxg2 18 ♝xg2 ♛d3+ 19
♚e1 winning. The gist of the analysis is that it is purely tactical, with
the only strategy being that White
should not retreat until he has made
major gains in material. White has a
winning attack if he pursues it properly, showing that Black dare not try
breakout manoeuvres against proper
System play. The latter point is very
important. At no point should White
have to make concessionary or defensive moves if he has played **System** moves all along. When Black
ventures 7...♝f5, this is a transgression. If this move were good, then 4
cxd5, allowing the c8-bishop out,
would have been a mistake. However, White's 4th is a **System** move;
therefore, 7...♝f5 must be an error
that is met aggressively. Under no
circumstances should White even
consider a move such as 8 ♝d3?,
which trades his good bishop for
Black's bad one.

After Six Moves in a Standard Line of Play

So now let us continue our example
of **The System** at work with a more
reasonable line of play for Black.

After 6 e3, Black can play 6...♗e7 *(D)*, which is one of the normal ways to continue. The black bishop has no other reasonable square, as he must break the pin in order to allow the f6-knight to participate more.

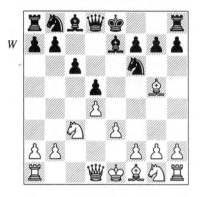

Let us now take stock, and see where we are going. White has a number of important advantages:

a) The majority of pawns in the centre.

b) The ability to control the e4-square while Black will not be able to control e5 in the near future.

c) Because of the way the pawns in the central area are fixed, White's f1-bishop is considerably better than its counterpart, the c8-bishop. The dark-squared bishops are nearly equal in value, since White has succeeded in getting his bishop to a meaningful post outside the pawn-chain, whereas Black's dark-squared bishop is unencumbered by its own pawns. However, Black's c8-bishop can at best hope for e6 (since ...♗f5 will be prevented) unless he wishes to indulge in ...♗g4, f3 ♗h5, which leaves the bishop vulnerable to attack by pawns and the manoeuvre ♘ge2-f4.

d) White is in a position eventually to advance his pawn majority in the centre.

The question is "How does one hold on to these advantages and move so that control over e4 remains with White, and he can eventually advance e4?" The plan is fairly obvious. It consists of the moves:

a) ♗d3 – Clearly the best square for this bishop.

b) ♘ge2 – Better than ♘f3, because the latter concedes control of the square e4. Also, this knight will work harmoniously with its colleague on c3.

c) 0-0 – The king must be sheltered, and the kingside has the only safe haven.

d) ♕c2 – The queen must be developed, and this is the right place. There is a little tactical trick involved in determining this. Let us say that some time in the future White plays a fully prepared e4. Then if the queen is still at d1, Black will be able to play ...♘xe4!, and in response to ♗xe7, reply ...♘xc3, thus also attacking the white queen and very likely winning a pawn. Therefore, the queen should go to c2, so it will not be attacked by ...♘xc3.

e) f3 – to control the e4-square and prepare the advance e4.

Black, on the other hand, has several defensive strategies:

a) Black can try to enforce ...♘e4, which would free his game if it could be done successfully. White has various ways of allowing ...♘e4 under unfavourable circumstances, or preventing it altogether.

b) Black can try to play ...♘a6 at a moment when White's queen is at c2 and bishop at d3, and thus threaten ...♘b4, and either force a wasted tempo with a3, whereupon the knight would continue to c7 and e6 with a reasonable location for participating in the fight, or have White give up his good bishop with ♗xa6.

c) If White plays ♕c2 without having first played ♗d3, Black could play ...g6 with the idea of proceeding ...♗f5. If this can be prevented by playing ♗d3, then Black has in mind to play ...♘bd7-f8-e6-g7 followed by ...♗f5. It is important to note that this manoeuvre can usually succeed in exchanging the bad bishop when White has his knight at f3, and is not able to challenge with f3 followed by e4. However, with the knight on e2, and f3 played, then Black's ...♗f5 is met with e4, which essentially refutes the whole manoeuvre.

d) Black can manoeuvre on the back two ranks to prepare an eventual freeing ...c5.

In the following discussion it might be helpful to refer to Chapter 2 in order to understand exactly what is being asserted. In particular, attention should be paid to the section (p.37) on **Response Pairs**. The above position could have been reached by Black playing first 5...♗e7 and then (after 6 e3) 6...c6. After 5...♗e7 6 e3, Black could also have chosen a number of other ways to proceed. He could have continued with either 6...0-0 or 6...♘bd7. He could not have played 6...♗f5 because then 7 ♗xf6 ♗xf6 8 ♕b3 wins a pawn.

What is important to notice, however, is that for the various plausible 6th moves for Black, the white response may be different. This is where the **Response Pairs** principle is invoked. Consider the following:

a) When Black plays 6...c6, he essentially gives up any idea of playing ...c5 soon as that would be a loss of a tempo. He defends the d5-pawn in order to threaten to play ...♘e4 or to get the c8-bishop out (so an eventual ♕b3 does not attack both the d5-pawn and the b7-pawn).

b) On the other hand, both 6...0-0 and 6...♘bd7 do not do anything to defend the d5-pawn, and thus the manoeuvre 7...♘e4 is not threatened as then would follow (after, for instance, 7 ♕c2) 8 ♗xe7 ♕xe7 9 ♘xd5. However, as long as Black has not played ...c6, he will be contemplating the immediate ...c5.

Since there is a difference in what 6...c6 threatens, and what other moves threaten, it is possible that White's best **System** move may be different for different moves, even though the same position may ultimately be reached by different pathways. That is what the **Response Pairs** Principle is about. It occurs in several **System** openings, and we will try to explain things as generally as possible.

Exactly how to Proceed

But which of the **System** moves is correct in the position of the previous diagram (repeated here for convenience)?

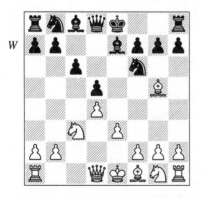

If Black had played ...♘bd7 or ...0-0 instead of ...c6, then 7 ♗d3 would be obviously correct since the bishop belongs there and **there is no threat of ...♘e4**. However, now Black has the threat of ...♘e4, and

we must consider whether we can meet the threat while still obeying the **System** principles. No thought should be given to 7 ♘f3, as this prematurely decides the position of the g1-knight.

The two moves from our strategic list that obey **System** logic best are 7 ♗d3 and 7 ♕c2. When playing ♕c2 before ♗d3, one must be careful about Black's possible ...♘a6. However, in this position, this is not the case. After 7 ♕c2, 7...♘a6 can be met by 8 ♗xa6 ruining Black's pawn structure and not losing any tempi by having had the bishop first move to d3. With 5...c6, Black opted for a particular set-up; one in which his playing ...c5 is not a consideration, and one in which ...♗f5 and ...♘e4 are major considerations that must be dealt with. 7 ♕c2 deals with them both, and postpones the developing move ♗d3 for one move. However, since Black is not exerting any pressure on the centre, this is fine.

Why 7 ♗d3 is not Correct

Let us look briefly at why 7 ♗d3 does not work. I have spent many hundreds of hours studying how White could play after 7...♘e4. White's next move is obvious; he plays 8 ♗xe7 and Black must reply 8...♕xe7 *(D)*, as after 8...♘xc3 9 ♗xd8 ♘xd1 10 ♔xd1! ♔xd8 11 b4! White has a very strong ending with a queenside minority attack under way, and by far the better bishop to boot. Black will only be able to sit idly by, while White strengthens his position.

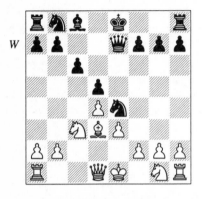

A Critical Position

So after 8 ♗xe7 ♕xe7 Black has obtained a free position at the cost of conceding the better bishop. White's only hope for an advantage is to continue 9 ♗xe4 dxe4 and then try to make capital by attacking the e4-pawn by 10 ♕c2 f5 or playing d5 somewhere. That neither of these ideas lead to any advantage has been borne out by much private analysis and tournament play (cf. Bronstein-Ståhlberg, Gothenburg 1954). However, the idea ♗xe4 certainly fits in with **System** play since the bishop is less valuable in a blocked position, and the knight more valuable. So if ♗xe4 makes a useful target out of the black e4-pawn, there is no real

investment by White. However, the circumstances must be right for exploiting this.

Because there is no way to take advantage of the black e4-pawn, the immediate 7 ♗d3 appears to be incorrect. Once one understands the **Response Pairs** principle, it is possible to see why the normal order of **System** moves may have to be altered.

The correct move is 7 ♕c2. With 7 ♕c2 White prevents Black's ...♘e4, since now 7...♘e4 8 ♗xe7 ♕xe7 9 ♘xd5 wins a pawn. Black can now try to show that 7 ♕c2 is premature by playing 7...g6. However, this does not work here, unlike the positions where White has already played ♘f3. Here White simply plays 8 ♗d3, after which the plan 8...♘a6 9 a3 ♘c7 10 ♘ge2 ♘e6 11 ♗h4 ♘g7 12 f3 ♗f5 (12...♘f5 13 ♗f2) 13 e4 fails for Black.

Black tries to enforce ...♘e4 without playing ...h6

It is better to try to force ...♘e4 after further preparation. Thus, 7...0-0 8 ♗d3, and now Black must make some decision about how to defend his h-pawn. A normal line of play that defends the h7-pawn and avoids weaknesses is 8...♘bd7 9 ♘ge2 ♖e8 10 0-0 *(D)*.

Now Black can try 10...♘e4, which is met by 11 ♗xe4! dxe4 (11...♗xg5

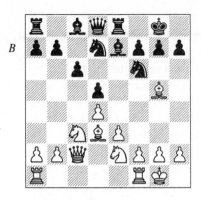

12 ♗xh7+) 12 ♗f4 f5 (the only way to defend the twice-attacked pawn) 13 ♘d5 *(D)*.

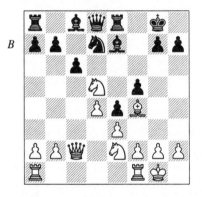

Now ♘c7 is threatened, and 13...cxd5 loses to 14 ♗c7.

Black plays ...h6

If Black had somewhere in the sequence leading to this position played ...h6 and thus induced the natural reply ♗h4, the h7-pawn would be moved and not subject to

attack. In that case, the above line starting with ♗xe4 would not work. There are advantages and disadvantages to ...h6. It weakens the kingside and in particular the g6-square, but it also removes the h7-pawn as a target and provides air for the black king. I am quite convinced that Black is better off avoiding playing ...h6.

If Black had played ...h6 somewhere in the sequence, we would then reach the position in the next diagram after White's 11 0-0 *(D)*.

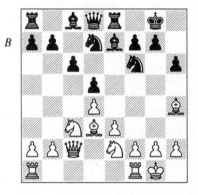

After 11 0-0;
Black has played ...h6

This position is the same as that in the last diagram but one, except the white bishop is at h4 and the black pawn is at h6.

If Black now plays 11...♘e4, then the refutation is somewhat different. It goes: 12 ♗xe7 ♕xe7 13 ♗xe4! (still the same logic) 13...dxe4 14

♘g3 ♘f6 15 h3!! (a move at the end of the opening, determined purely by tactical considerations; now Black will be unable to play ...♗g4 at a later time, and White can proceed with the attack f3). At this point Black has two possible lines of play *(D)*:

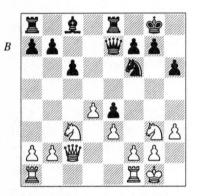

a) 15...b6 16 f3! ♗a6 (if 16...exf3 17 ♖xf3 ♗a6, 18 ♘f5 is very strong) 17 fxe4!! ♗xf1 18 ♖xf1 and White's attack beginning with e5 is very strong whereas Black really has no good activity for his rooks.

b) 15...c5! 16 ♖fd1! b6 17 dxc5 ♕xc5 (17...bxc5 18 ♘a4 ♘d7 19 ♖ac1 wins the c-pawn) 18 ♖d4! ♗b7 (18...♗f5 19 ♖ad1 ♗g6 is worse) 19 ♖ad1 and White's pieces dominate the board. He controls the d-file whereas Black can get nowhere on the c-file because the c3-knight is securely anchored.

Since neither of these lines is satisfactory for Black, we can safely conclude that 11...♘e4 does not work. The above analysis is a major contribution of this book, as it refutes this freeing method.

One other possibility to get in the freeing ...♘e4 is the following sequence: 7 ♕c2 0-0 8 ♗d3 h6 9 ♗h4 ♖e8 10 ♘ge2 ♘e4 *(D)*.

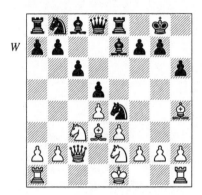

Here Black has omitted ...♘bd7 and White has not yet castled. This means that if the e4-pawn needs attention, Black must use his f-pawn to defend it. So the refutation goes 11 ♗xe7 ♕xe7 12 ♗xe4 dxe4 13 ♘g3 f5 (it is not possible to defend the e4-pawn indirectly; for instance, after 13...♔h8; White can simply play 14 0-0 and Black must again face the problem of defending the e4-pawn). However, White now simply plays 14 0-0 ♘a6 15 f3! ♘b4 (after 15...exf3 16 ♖xf3 g6 17 e4 Black's position is in ruins) 16 ♕d2, and Black again faces hopeless problems as his kingside is full of holes.

Therefore, this method of proceeding by Black to force through ...♘e4 at the earliest moment is not to be recommended.

The Manoeuvring Defence

In the position after 10 0-0 *(diagram repeated here)*, Black must eschew the breakout, and play a conservative move.

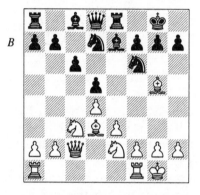

10...♘f8 is best here, when White begins his central advance with 11 f3. The best reply then is 11...♘g6!, solidifying the king's position. Black has played in a Steinitz-like manner, avoiding any weakening, and now awaits whatever action White will take. Now White proceeds with 12 e4 dxe4 (Black cannot allow e5 at this point) 13 fxe4 ♗e6! (the attempt to counter-attack with 13...c5 would lose to 14 ♗xf6 ♗xf6 15 ♘d5 ♗xd4+ 16 ♘xd4 cxd4 17 ♘c7) bringing us to the following position *(D)*.

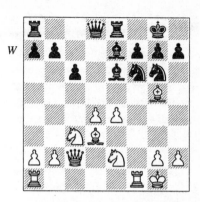

After 13 moves in the Manoeuvring Defence

We are in a position from Berliner-Zagorovsky, 5th World Correspondence Ch Final, 1965-8. White has executed his plan to control the centre and then advance his pawns into it. Black has taken a position with no weaknesses, but somewhat cramped.

White's position seems ideal. All his pieces except the undeveloped a1-rook are on ideal squares. He controls a lot of space, and his centre is strong. However, Black's position is really quite solid, and if White were to have to move his d-pawn, then the e5-square would fall into Black's hands giving him an ideal location for a bishop or knight, and making the white d3-bishop into a weakling. So Black's threat of ...c5 is very real. It would seem, at first glance, that White can play e5 and exchange bishops with a very superior game. However, 14 e5 is met by 14...♞g4, and if the bishops are exchanged this knight will threaten to invade on the dark squares. If not, then ...c5 will be played with strong effect for Black. So White must make a critical decision about how to proceed.

In the above cited game, I played 14 ♗xf6, which, together with 15 e5, creates a positional character favouring the light-squared bishop. The fact that the game was drawn made me criticize 14 ♗xf6, and 14 h3 has been suggested as an improvement. However, 14 h3 really does not work. For instance, after 14...c5 15 ♗xf6 ♗xf6 16 e5 cxd4 17 exf6 dxc3 Black's position is quite sound.

There is no doubt that White has the preferable position in the above diagram. He has a major space advantage. He dominates a fluid centre that can be turned into a form that he desires in order to enhance the power of one of his bishops. However, he must act **now**. Re-examining the play in the above-quoted game leisurely and with the help of computers, it is now quite clear to me that White did not make the very best of his chances. After 14 ♗xf6! ♗xf6 15 e5 ♗e7 16 ♖ad1 ♗f8 *(D)*

White stands considerably better, and must only be careful not to let Black's bishops become too active.

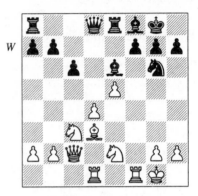

If a position were reached in which both light-squared bishops were exchanged, the remaining black bishop would have great difficulty in finding fertile areas to dominate, while the white knights are very strong and in a position to invade the squares on the kingside and places such as d6.

That one can demonstrate such a domination of an opening that has been a stand-by for many decades shows that there is a lot to **The System**. There are many lines we have not delved into, but these are the principal lines of play and in each case, **The System** appears to be able to maintain a clear advantage.

5 The King's Fianchetto Defences

The System and Hypermodern Chess

There are a number of sections of this book devoted to defences that start with 1 d4 d5. However, most players today prefer the defences starting with 1 d4 ♘f6 which allow a number of 'minimum contact' openings in which Black can prepare his plans without always being in a position of having to defend his centre.

One of the non-contact approaches, the hypermodern, originated in the 1920s. This method allows one's opponent to occupy and control the centre with his pawns in the hope of later using these opposing pawns as targets and bringing the whole structure down with a well-timed attack.

Needless to say, themes in hypermodern openings are much more complex. This is because the side occupying the centre is trying to increase his stranglehold without creating a critical weakening. The more restricted opponent is manoeuvring his pieces into positions that offer great potential for an effective counter-attack. This means he must keep as many potential targets in mind as possible. He must be alert for the opportunity to counter, while not allowing himself to get into a passive position while waiting.

Needless to say, **The System**, with its strong advocacy of board control, feels very much at home against openings of this type. **The System** advocates making moves that control critical squares. In the process, moves that weaken squares and make targets of pawns are omitted. So White, using **System** strategies, will build up a strong centre that can withstand all counter-attacks.

In this chapter, we examine the hypermodern defences that grow out of the king's fianchetto, the Grünfeld and the King's Indian. After 1 d4 ♘f6 2 c4, 2...g6 *(D)* ushers in the king's fianchetto defences.

The bishop will be placed so that it bears indirectly on the centre and could later have great activity there. In this position, White should now play the obvious **System** move 3 ♘c3, and proceed directly with his quest to control the centre. Yet it is amazing to see how many good players still play 3 g3 in this position.

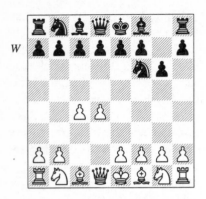

later, or the Grünfeld Defence with 3...d5 which places a pawn in the centre, but only with the idea of giving up the centre later anyway. We shall examine the Grünfeld Defence first.

The Grünfeld Defence

The Grünfeld begins with the moves 1 d4 ♘f6 2 c4 g6 3 ♘c3 d5 *(D)*.

The reason for this is not always clear. They may fear the Grünfeld Defence, but by avoiding 3 ♘c3 they give Black many opportunities for achieving equality. Anyone who has read to this point will recognize that 3 g3 cannot be correct as it commits the bishop before it is possible to determine whether it should stay on its original diagonal (where it defends the c4-pawn), or not. Therefore, it is not surprising to see that when White plays 3 g3, his opening advantage disappears shortly against proper play, and that Black usually gets counterplay against the pawn on c4, which can easily become weak without its natural protection.

Also, 3 ♘f3, which also avoids the Grünfeld, cannot possibly be correct, as it gives up control over e4, as has been explained previously. After 3 ♘c3, Black must decide on whether to play the popular King's Indian Defence with 3...♗g7 which leaves contesting for the centre until

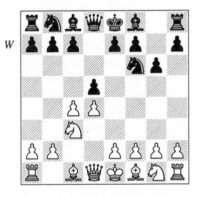

It is easy to determine that each of White's first three moves are **System** moves as described in earlier chapters. In this position, there are a variety of 'book' moves: 4 ♘f3, 4 ♗f4, 4 e3, 4 ♕b3, 4 ♗g5, and 4 cxd5. However, all the above moves, except 4 ♕b3 and 4 cxd5, evade the basic question posed by Black's central thrust.

The problems associated with Black's unsupported centre will have to be faced sooner or later. We have learned that the sooner such problems are resolved, the more readily we can place our pieces correctly. However, of our two alternatives we should be wary of 4 ♕b3 as this commits the queen at a time when it is not at all clear where it really belongs. Thus, after 4...dxc4 5 ♕xc4 ♗e6 6 ♕b5+ ♘c6 Black already has a very good game. It is interesting that the books uniformly pooh-pooh this line as bad. I can remember as a child around 1945, that this was one of the main lines. It was never clear to me why this should be bad for Black, and still today it seems the reason it is bad, is that everyone in authority says it is bad; copying one from another. But in reality, after 7 ♘f3 (not 7 ♕xb7 ♘xd4) 7...♘d5! 8 e4 (8 ♕xb7 ♘db4) 8...a6! (not in any book I know of) 9 ♕a4 (9 ♕e2 ♘xc3 10 bxc3 ♗g7 and Black looks OK; or 9 ♕xb7 ♘db4) 9...♘xc3 10 bxc3 ♗g7 *(D)*, and Black looks fine with a lead in development that gives him easy play.

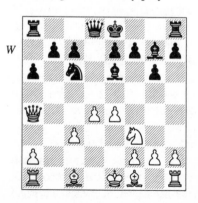

This line already shows to what an extent White is exposing himself with the risky and premature 4 ♕b3. There are other lines for Black that are also not bad, although Black must fight for equality.

However, the natural and **Systemic** move 4 cxd5 is correct, and leads to the variation 4...♘xd5 5 e4 ♘xc3 6 bxc3 *(D)*.

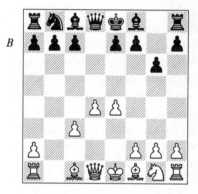

Now, there are two basic paths that Black may choose:

a) The immediate counter-attack involving the advance ...c5 on move 6, 7, or 8.

b) Slow variations, in which Black hopes that White will make a move that allows a successful counter-attack.

We first take up the counter-attack approach, because of the fact that in other lines there is frequently the possibility of transposing back to this line.

The Immediate Counter-Attack with ...c5

After 6...c5, the point of Black's plan initiated with 3...d5 becomes clear. He intends to lay siege to White's d4-pawn, and can still bring a knight and bishop to help do this. Therefore, White plans to deploy his forces so as to give this pawn two more units of protection. These must come from the c1-bishop and the g1-knight. Obviously the c1-bishop should go to e3, from where it affects the centre while retaining control over its original diagonal. However, with the g1-knight it is not that easy; at f3 it has fine scope but is subject to pin and capture by ...♗g4, while at e2 it has less scope but is safe from the pin because of the reply f3.

We first examine the 7 ♘f3 *(D)* variation.

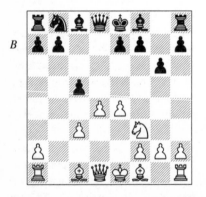

This could possibly be a **System** move if it were not for the previously noted fact that this knight is needed to defend the centre pawn on d4. If the knight goes to f3, it will later be pinned by ...♗g4, and then the white centre would be under severe pressure. Therefore, it is unlikely that this move is correct, but let us check it out. White plays 7 ♘f3, and then comes 7...♗g7 8 ♗e3 ♘c6. The order of White's moves is not important (which is a good reason for suspecting they are not **System** moves), but we are now at a critical point for White. White must face up to the threat of ...♗g4, which would destroy his centre. The best way to do this is by 9 ♗c4 which prevents 9...♗g4 due to 10 ♗xf7+. However, Black simply continues 9...♕a5 10 ♕d2 cxd4 11 cxd4 ♕xd2+ 12 ♔xd2 0-0, and now the threat of ...♗g4 and ...♖d8 assures Black of a good game.

These variations make it clear that White's position would be much more cohesive if the knight were at e2 and not exposed to the pin, because ...♗g4 would be met by f3. However, if the knight is going to e2, the f1-bishop must get out first. Clearly, there is only one good square for it, so the main line proceeds 7 ♗c4 ♗g7 8 ♘e2 (the knight definitely belongs here, while we cannot be sure about the c1-bishop yet) 8...♘c6 9 ♗e3 0-0 *(D)*.

This turns out to be an extremely important theoretical position, and one from which much can be learned.

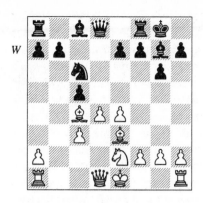

White to Play: Critical Position in the Grünfeld Defence

White is firmly in control of the centre, and must now decide what to do next. The opening books are unanimous in recommending 10 0-0. However, strangely enough, Black can just about force a draw after that move by simply playing 10...cxd4 11 cxd4 ♞a5 (D).

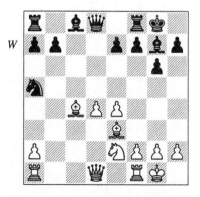

After 12 ♝d3 ♞c6! White has nothing better than 13 ♝c4. This is

best because any move such as 13 ♝c2 would allow Black control over c4, and remove the bishop from its important a2-g8 diagonal, on which it performs many functions. Another alternative in this line is for White to play 12 ♜c1, whereupon 12...♞xc4 13 ♜xc4 ♝d7 yields Black a fine game. White is without his bishop-pair, and his slight space advantage is not worth much without good minor pieces. Bronstein's sacrificial line, 13 d5!?, is taken up below. However, it has been analysed to a draw. Thus, the whole 10 0-0 line of play is hardly to be recommended for White.

However, the books continue in their error of recommending 10 0-0. Classical theory teaches us that when one side dominates the centre and controls more space, then he must attack. The question is where White is to attack. On the queenside, there are no targets. To advance the centre pawns only gives Black's pieces more scope. However, there is a target on the kingside, the black g-pawn, which can be attacked thematically by h4-h5. However, if this attack is correct then 10 0-0 is certainly not correct as it removes the h1-rook from a vital post.

I once discussed this position with David Bronstein, who pioneered the wonderful attack (after 10 0-0 cxd4 11 cxd4 ♞a5 12 ♝d3 ♞c6 13 d5!? ♝xa1 14 ♛xa1) which though brilliant was found only to lead to a draw with the best defence by Black. I said to David "Why would anyone want to castle in this position? What good is the rook going to do on the squares b1 through f1?". David looked at me in his wonderful way, and said nothing. That was quite a statement. Clearly, this idea had made an impression on a connoisseur of this opening.

I played 10 h4?! *(D)* in many games during the 1960s with unclear results.

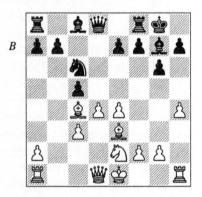

I played it three times in the 5th World Correspondence Championship (1965-8) that I won, and was lucky to get two points out of the three games. A game with the Soviet GM G. Borisenko continued 10...cxd4 11 cxd4 b5? 12 ♗d5 ♗d7 13 h5 e6 14 ♗b3 ♘a5 15 ♕d2 ♘b7 (Black would like to exchange queens; after 15...♘xb3 16 axb3, the attack commencing with ♗h6 and hxg6 is unstoppable) 16 ♖c1 ♖c8 17 ♖xc8 and

now after 17...♗xc8 18 hxg6 fxg6 (or 18...hxg6 19 ♔f1!! ♕a5 20 ♕c1 and the attack starting with ♗h6 is overwhelming) 19 ♘f4 White could expect to win quickly. Black's 11th move was far from best and constituted a loss of valuable time. The opponents in the other two games played much better, and I was lucky to escape with draws. This convinced me that 10 h4 is incorrect. Now, we will reveal the correct **System** move.

The **System** and winning move is 10 ♖c1 *(D)*.

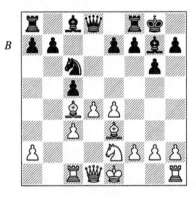

Why is this move correct? Firstly, it passes the important **System** test of not allowing the drawing line 10...♘a5, which is now met by 11 ♗d3 cxd4 (the immediate 11...♘c6 is met with 12 d5 winning a pawn) 12 cxd4 ♘c6 and now the wonderful innovation 13 ♖c5! *(D)*.

This defends White's d-pawn indirectly in a most unusual way. If

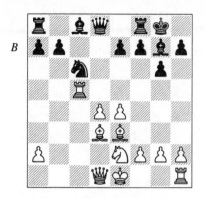

now 13...②xd4, 14 ☐d5 wins, and 13...e6 (13...♗e6 14 d5! wins) 14 ♗b1, and now White has everything his way. The move 10 ☐c1, which makes possible 13 ☐c5!, is one of the major 'theoretical' contributions of this book.

10 ☐c1 is the **only** move that avoids the above drawing line. On the face of it, 10 ☐c1 appears to be a wasted move, but it solidifies the queenside against any coming attacks and thus allows White to concentrate all his forces on the coming attack against the black king.

I discovered the above about 1976, having retired from active competition, and being able to devote time to such research. However, this move has since been introduced into tournament play by Lev Polugaevsky in 1987. I make no claim here for being the originator of the move, since tournament practice must hold sway over unpublished analysis. However, what is important is whether 10

☐c1 is the **System** move in this position. Below, we present strong evidence that it is, and that, despite being currently in disrepute among the top players, it is in actuality a winning continuation.

What can Black play against 10 ☐c1 ?

At the time I discovered 10 ☐c1, I based my judgement of its effectiveness primarily on the fact that it prevented the drawing manoeuvre, and thus made it possible to continue with the attack h4-h5, which I had played prematurely on move 10 in three games in the 5th World Correspondence Championship Final. I thought that White will play ♔f1 in response to ...♕a5(+) and thereafter pursue his attack with efficiency. It was not realistic to analyse much more than that. Now, however, that the move has been tested in many GM games, and, strangely, the world has a poor opinion of it, it was possible to apply **System** principles to the various attempts to refute 10 ☐c1 and see what can be found.

Let us look at how Black can continue. He must act on the queenside before the attack against the king with h4 gets too strong (strangely in several games by top players with this variation, White chickens out, and plays 0-0). It follows that Black must either pressure the centre with

...♕a5 or expand on the queenside with ...♘a5.

Defences based upon ...♕a5
In some people's eyes, 10...♕a5 (threatening 11...cxd4) would appear to force 11 0-0 anyway. However, this is wrong! White simply answers 11 ♔f1!! *(D)*, which is based upon much of the earlier discussion.

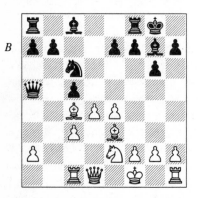

White intends to continue with h4-h5, and with the centre secure, the attack on the black king will proceed with overwhelming energy.

A game Browne-Wolff, US Ch 1992, which is critical to an appraisal of the whole 10 ♖c1 idea, continued correctly 11 ♔f1 b5 12 ♗d5 ♗b7 13 h4! e6 14 ♗b3 ♖fd8 (the idea of 14...c4 15 ♗c2 ♕xa2 in this and similar positions is not to be recommended; for Black to have some say in what is going to happen, he must challenge the centre, and winning the a-pawn will expedite White's attack

on the black king, which will succeed long before the a-pawn becomes a queen) 15 h5 cxd4 16 cxd4 ♕b4 *(D)*.

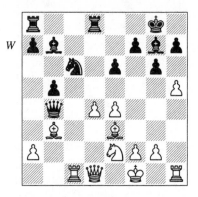

White's moves to this point have all clearly been **System** moves, pursuing his objectives simply and purposefully. However, now Black is putting the question to the white centre, and it behoves White to play ultra-correctly to demonstrate the correctness of his previous play.

This can be done by 17 hxg6! which forces 17...hxg6 as otherwise the white attack gets much too strong. Now comes the beautiful denouement: 18 d5 which threatens to win a piece with 19 ♗d2. Black almost certainly had prepared the move 18...♕xe4 here, but that loses to 19 ♘g3!! ♕e5 (there is no other move) 20 ♕g4!! exd5 (what else can be done?) 21 ♕h4 *(D)* and White's attack is very strong:

a) On 21...d4, 22 ♕h7+ ♔f8 23 ♗h6 wins at least a piece.

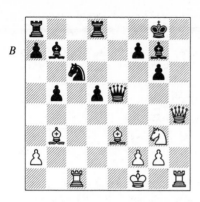

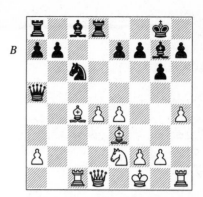

b) On 21...♘d4!, 22 ♗f4 ♕f6 23 ♗g5 ♕b6 24 ♘e4! ♖dc8 25 ♖e1 leaves Black in terrible shape. He cannot play 25...dxe4 26 ♕h7+ ♔f8 27 ♗h6; nor can he capture with 25...♘xb3, because 26 ♘f6+ ♔f8 27 ♕h8+! mates in four. So, he must play 25...♘f5 26 ♕h7+ ♔f8 27 g4 dxe4 28 gxf5 gxf5 29 ♗h6 with an attack that wins a piece.

c) The other alternative, 21...♖ac8 22 ♖e1 ♕c3 23 ♘e2 ♕b2 24 ♗c5 f6 25 ♘f4, is also hopeless for Black. These lines are exquisite and difficult enough to find so that one can safely say that not even the strongest players in the world would have found them over the board without previous home analysis. However, they are very convincing proof of the strength of White's position.

After 10...♕a5 11 ♔f1, Black can also try 11...cxd4 12 cxd4 ♖d8, but then 13 h4! is strong (D):

a) 13...♕a3 14 ♖c3 ♕d6 15 h5 ♘xd4 16 ♘xd4 ♗xd4 17 ♖d3 e5 18

hxg6 hxg6 (18...♕xg6 19 ♗xd4 exd4 20 ♖g3) 19 ♕f3 ♕e7 (19...♗e6 20 ♕f6, or 19...♖f8 20 ♗g5) 20 ♗xf7+ ♔g7 (20...♕xf7 22 ♖h8+) 21 ♗xg6 ♔xg6 22 ♕h5+ wins.

b) If instead 13...h5 then 14 ♕b3! e6 (14...♘xd4 15 ♗xf7+ ♔h7 16 ♘xd4 ♗xd4 17 ♗xd4 ♖xd4 18 ♗g8+ ♔ any 19 ♕f7 and mates; also, if 14...♖f8, then 15 ♗d5! is very strong) 15 e5!!, and now Black can only sit passively by while White controls the board. For instance, 15...♕b4 16 ♗g5 and Black must retreat. White's h1-rook will be developed via h3, and Black is essentially helpless.

The only other meaningful defence is based upon following up on ...♕a5 with ...♗d7 and a general deployment on the queenside, hoping to gain the upper hand on the light squares before White's attack becomes too strong. The line 10...cxd4 11 cxd4 ♕a5+ 12 ♔f1 ♗d7 was played in a game Shirov-Kožul, Biel

1991, which continued 13 h4 ♖fc8 14 h5 ♘d8 (to steady the kingside and put pressure on c4). White can now simply play 15 hxg6 hxg6 (D).

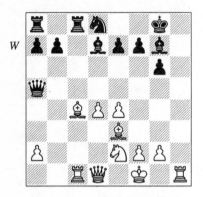

How is White to Proceed?

The play to here clearly conforms exactly to **System** principles. So White should have an effective continuation here. In fact, when I first saw this position, I could not believe that this was considered a serious defence. White's pieces are all deployed beautifully, and Black still has a long way to go. It is instructive to examine it in detail.

White appears to have a very strong attacking position. If he could only get his queen on the c1-h6 diagonal or on the h-file, he would get an overwhelming attack with ♗h6. However, that plan is difficult to implement in the present position. Further, if Black can exchange the light-squared bishops, he will have

excellent play on the queenside. So what is White to do? With all his pieces basically deployed to great effect, a **System** move must be one that moves forward seriously to the attack. White has many potential **System** moves:

a) 16 e5 or 16 d5, which both gain space and keep the black queen from the kingside.

b) 16 ♕d3, which mobilizes the queen to a slightly better square and has certain ideas for moving it to the kingside for attack. This move also prevents ...♗b5, which is exactly what Black is trying to play.

c) 16 f3, which steadies the centre and may make possible a sequence such as ♗d2 and ♕e1-h4.

d) 16 ♗h6, which aims to exchange Black's best defensive piece.

16 f4 cannot be the **System** move as it weakens the light squares around the white king too much without f5 being much of a threat. This position has now occurred many times in GM play, but to the best of my knowledge no one found the correct **System** move from the selection given above. Despite the fact that Shirov, who is certainly an exceptionally strong attacking player, has played the position after Black's 14th more than once, he failed to find the correct continuation.

After becoming aware of the current 'theory' with respect to this position, I spent over 50 hours studying it. White's pieces occupy near-optimal positions, so it is not clear which of the above candidate moves is correct. 16 ♗h6 appears premature as after 16...♗xh6 White must play 17 ♖xh6 and the future cooperation between rook and queen seems in doubt. However, White must proceed rapidly as moves such as e5, d5, or f3 are much too slow, and the natural-appearing 16 ♕d3 is answered by 16...a6! (suggested by B. Lalić in *The Grünfeld for the Attacking Player*), whereupon ...♗b5 can no longer be prevented. I did spend quite a bit of time investigating 16 ♕d3 a6 (after 16...b5 17 ♗d5 White has a very strong position) 17 ♖b1! ♗b5!? 18 ♖xb5!! axb5 19 ♗b3, whereupon White has a strong attack, but sufficient defence can be found by a capable computer.

However, 16 ♗h6! *(D)* is correct!!

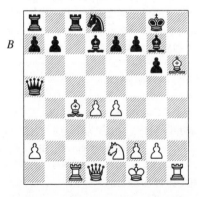

Black has several possible defences, the most active one being

16...♗xh6 17 ♖xh6 ♕g5 18 ♖h2. Now, Black must essentially continue with 18...b5, as 18...♗b5 19 f4 wins a piece. After 18...b5 play continues 19 f4 ♕g4 (on 19...♕f6 20 e5 ♕f5, 21 ♔f2!! with the threat of ♕h1 wins, and 20...♕g7 leaves Black in a pitiable state) 20 ♗d5 ♖xc1 (20...♗c6 loses immediately to 21 ♗xc6 ♖xc6 22 ♖xc6 ♘xc6 23 d5) 21 ♕xc1 ♖c8 22 ♕d2 ♗c6 (22...e6 23 ♗b3 leaves Black totally bankrupt with a bad bishop, and queen in danger of being trapped) with the following position *(D)*:

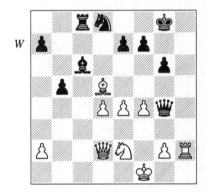

23 f5!! gxf5 (needed to deal with the threat of ♕h6) 24 ♖h3! ♗xd5 25 exd5!! f4! 26 ♘xf4 ♘b7 27 ♘h5! ♕f5+ 28 ♔g1 ♕xd5 29 ♕e3!!! with the amazing threat of ♘f4 followed by ♕g3+ winning. Neither I nor my computer could find any defence in this position.

There are other potential defences for Black after 16 ♗h6, and it would be premature to pronounce Black as being lost. However, 16...♗b5 cannot be played because of 17 ♗xb5 ♗xh6 (17...♕xb5 18 ♗xg7 ♔xg7 19 ♕d2 is overwhelming) 18 ♖xc8 ♖xc8 19 ♗d7 ♖c7 20 ♖xh6 ♖xd7 21 ♕b3 with overwhelming threats on the kingside, e.g. 21...♕a6 22 ♕h3 ♖xd4 23 ♖h8+ ♔g7 24 ♕h6+ ♔f6 25 e5+ ♔xe5 (25...♔e6 26 ♕h3+ comes to the same thing) 26 ♕e3+ ♖e4 27 f4+ and the rook is lost.

Another try is 16...♗xh6 17 ♖xh6 ♔g7!? *(D).*

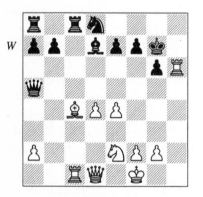

But after 18 ♖h4! (it is important to keep the option of using the rook in front of the pawns) 18...♘c6 (after 18...♕g5 19 ♖h2 the position is like the one analysed above, except that the king is more exposed on g7) 19 ♖f4! f6 20 e5 ♖h8 21 ♔g1 and now White has a very strong initiative in the centre (e6) and on the kingside despite the fact that the h-file has changed hands. Also, Black

is unable to play 18...♗b5 in view of 19 ♗xb5 ♕xb5 20 ♕d2 with a winning attack for White. So Black is reduced to purely defensive moves and White is very strongly placed.

Lines where Black plays ...♘a5

The line 10...♘a5 is a natural defence, but it fails to put sufficient pressure on the centre. Black will, indeed, drive the c4-bishop off its most important diagonal, but the attack h4-h5 proceeds anyway and Black has no meaningful play against d4 and must content himself with relatively meaningless gestures against the queenside.

A typical continuation would be 10...♘a5 11 ♗d3 ♗d7 (there is no better move: 11...e5 is met by 12 dxe5; and 11...cxd4 12 cxd4 gives White everything he could ask for in the centre while the c8-bishop still has no better square than d7). These lines make it quite clear that if Black is to survive here, he must play a line involving ...♕a5.

Other passive lines

The move 10...♗d7 has been suggested, but this is very slow. White simply plays 11 h4! ♕a5 (on 11...h5, 12 ♘f4 is very strong; and on 11...♘a5 12 ♗d3 it is hard to suggest anything for Black as 12...e5 is met simply by 13 dxe5) 12 h5 b5 13 ♗d5! e6 14 ♗b3 cxd4 15 ♘xd4 and Black's counterplay is very slow and weak.

If Black does not react strongly, White will continue with the attack h4-h5 as previously explained. With the very difficult to find introductory move 10 ♖c1!, which defends the centre, everything else proceeds according to plan.

In Summary

We have gone to great lengths to assure that all the above is valid.

a) All the moves do qualify as **System** moves as set down in this book.

b) The analysis has been carefully checked by computer and other qualified players.

Although it is somewhat early to make the following claim (as one should allow time for testing in GM practice), I believe that the above analyses basically refute the main line of the Grünfeld Defence.

The Slow Variations

Therefore, the only meaningful course for Black, if he wishes to play the Grünfeld, would be to play one of the variations that does not immediately counter-attack with 6...c5. In this, White must be continuously wary of transposition into the main line where one or more of his pieces have been misplaced. Thus, the **transposition rule** comes into play a great deal. For instance, if after 6

bxc3, Black plays 6...♗g7 instead of 6...c5, then we certainly have enough understanding to know that we should now play 7 ♗c4, as this would lead after 7...c5 to the same position as if Black had transposed his 6th and 7th moves.

However, things will not remain that simple. White must develop his position:

a) According to **System** principles;

b) Taking into account that Black may transpose into the counter-attack variation at any time;

c) Yet developing his attack against the kingside in such a way as to take into account the two constraints above.

The observant reader may have noticed that the lines against the Grünfeld are full of examples of the **Response Pairs** principle. We now restate the principle, first defined in Chapter 2, p.37, and then go to examples. The **Response Pairs** principle states:

There may be openings in which certain moves are required as responses to Black's moves. This will result in pairings of the type: black move → white reply.

This will almost always be because the black move prepares some counter-attack, and the **response** is the **System** way of preventing it. There may be several counter-attacks, and each will have its own **response**.

Let us see how this works for the analysis just concluded. According to the **Options** principle, White would ideally like to develop his pieces in the following way:

a) First, ♗c4 as this is where the bishop belongs, and it takes no options away from any other piece.

b) Second, ♘e2 as the knight belongs here to avoid the pin ...♗g4, and because it is still not clear where the c1-bishop should go.

c) Third, the c1-bishop when it is clear where it should go.

However, the **Response Pairs** principle intervenes to change this order at times. These are the issues:

a) Black's ...c5 must be answered by ♗e3 (unless it is already there). This is so the c1-square becomes free for the a1-rook in case of ...♕c7 threatening ...cxd4. There is an exception to this rule, and that occurs when Black plays 6...c5. Then, we can play 7 ♗c4 because now 7...♕c7 is answered by 8 ♕b3, forcing a major weakness with the forced reply 8...e6.

b) White must be prepared to defend the d4-pawn as many times as it is attacked. However, since it is defended by a pawn, Black's attacks are meaningless unless ...c5 is part of the attack. So as long as ...c5 has been (or is ready to be) played White must be able to counter:

b1) ...c5 with ♗e3;

b2) ...♘c6 with ♘e2;

b3) ...♗g7 with ♗c4.

c) However, if Black were to block the c7-pawn before it can advance, then the defence of the d4-pawn is securely in the hands of the c3-pawn, and the above rules need not be invoked. In a line such as 6...♗g7 7 ♗c4 0-0 8 ♘e2 ♘c6, it would appear that White should now turn his attention to where to attack, since the centre is no longer in danger. However, this is not quite true, since Black can at some future time play ...♘a5 followed by ...c5 when the white bishop moves. So the **Response Pairs** rules remain valid after 8...♘c6. However, if Black were to choose some deployment starting with the fianchetto ...b6, which loses a move in the attack on the centre without any transposition possibilities, White would now be free to start his attack.

d) Although it will not come out in this analysis, except possibly in unmentioned sidelines, it is necessary that any time Black plays ...f5 that this be met by an immediate e5, which will hopelessly cramp Black and leave his dark squares very weak.

There is one more thing that needs to be said about the slow variations of the Grünfeld. If White castles, then his attack against the king via h4-h5 disappears. Thus, Black's main hope is that White will castle, and the game will turn into a positional struggle. However, having seen that the attack will carry the day, even in the face of aggressive counter-action in the centre, it should be clear that White should just proceed with his kingside attack and forego castling.

Now let us go into detail about the correct **System** lines in the slow variation (omitting 6...c5). The reason we first examined the immediate counter-attack by Black is that it forms the basis of how the play will go given the **transposition** rule and the set of **Response Pairs**. If Black does not take aggressive counter-measures, but makes a move that could fit into some future counter, then White must play in such a way as to be able to transpose to known **System** positions.

Thus, Black's slow development will hinge on one of two ideas. Either, he will play ...♞c6 with the idea of at some point playing ...♞a5 and after White plays ♗d3, then ...c5. Or he will play ...b6 with slow pressure on the centre. In both cases the preliminary moves 6...♗g7 7 ♗c4 0-0 8 ♞e2 will first be played. Now Black can continue 8...♞c6, when 9 ♗e3! must be played in order to answer 9...♞a5 10 ♗d3 c5 with 11 ♖c1!, when we are back in one of the main lines. So Black usually plays 9...b6, when the attack with 10 h4! *(D)* can begin.

Black has no long-term hope of countering this. If 10...♞a5 11 ♗d3

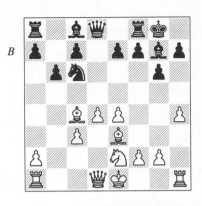

e5, then 12 h5 ♛e7 13 ♛d2 exd4 14 cxd4 ♗b7 15 f3 and White stands clearly superior. One possibility is 15...c5 16 ♗h6 ♗xh6 17 ♛xh6 cxd4 18 e5! with a very strong attack. Clearly the position after 13 ♛d2 *(D)* is full of possibilities. However, White has played correctly to this point, and the dynamics favour him. I would feel confident to play this in a correspondence game where one had (say) a week to work on each move.

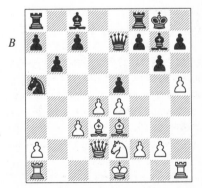

If above instead of 9...b6 Black plays 9...e5, then 10 ♕d2 gets into all the correct transpositions.

Also, 8...b6 is met by the immediate 9 h4, which resulted in a convincing win for White with the further 9...e5 10 h5 exd4 11 hxg6 hxg6 12 cxd4 ♕e7 13 ♕b3! in de Carbonnel-Messere, 5th World Correspondence Ch Final, 1965-8.

One Last Variation

One other variation still needs attention. Suppose Black plays 5...♘b6 instead of 5...♘xc3. Here the books in their typical insipid manner recommend 6 h3, so that the centre can be defended without allowing the pin ...♗g4. However, it would seem that White should be able to do that without wasting time with such a silly move. The problem relates to where to deploy the f1-bishop. The best square for this bishop is c4, and that has now been denied. So where is the bishop to be placed? According to the theory of options it is not at all clear where it should go. On d3 it blocks the defence of the d-pawn from behind, and on e2 it is really not accomplishing anything it does not do on f1. Maybe, we should wait before deploying the bishop, and see if there is another way to proceed.

White can develop while defending his centre with 6 ♗e3! ♗g7 7 ♕d2! ♘c6 8 0-0-0 (D).

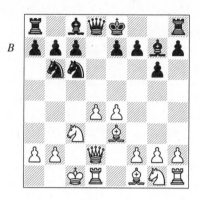

Now his centre is completely secure, and he can proceed with a kingside attack starting with h4.

While it has not been possible to deal with every variation in this analysis of the slow variations, I believe the major lines have been dealt with adequately. Once White is able to play h4-h5, he has a strong attack, and unless his centre has been weakened in the process, he should be able to carry the day with the kingside attack.

The King's Indian Defence

What is the Correct Development Plan?

After the moves 1 d4 ♘f6 2 c4 g6 3 ♘c3 ♗g7 4 e4 d6 (D), the weakest point in White's pawn structure is the pawn at d4, which cannot be defended by either of its neighbours.

With his last move Black served notice that he intends eventually to

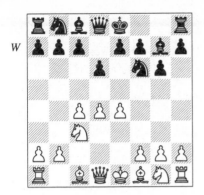

challenge that pawn and particularly **the square it is on** with either ...c5 or ...e5. Now it is important to note that if White were to answer such a challenge by either capturing the challenging pawn or advancing d5, Black would be left in full control of the d4-square, and that is essentially the main point of Black's strategy. True, if White chooses to play d5 it is unlikely that Black will ever get a knight to d4. But that is not as important as the fact that the square will not be available to the white pieces themselves. Therefore, it would seem a superior strategy for White to be able to meet the coming attack on his d4-pawn by being prepared to defend it with pieces as often as necessary to maintain the tension.

If White can maintain his d4-pawn by adequately defending it without otherwise compromising his position, the play will turn in his favour since he already controls most of the light squares in the centre. Very importantly, move 5 is the time when White must make key decisions as to how to deploy his pieces. It's therefore not surprising that very many alternatives have been tried in this position in master play: 5 ♘f3, 5 ♗e2, 5 f3, 5 f4, 5 ♗g5, 5 ♗d3, 5 ♘ge2, 5 g3, and 5 h3. We will first examine this list to see which of the above moves qualify as possible **System** moves.

a) 5 ♘f3 cannot be right because it blocks the f-pawn in a situation in which it is not at all clear whether that pawn has a role to play in the fight for the centre.

b) 5 ♗e2 just can't be right. Why move that bishop to that square? It is not clear where the bishop belongs, and this is very premature.

c) 5 f3 and 5 f4 are both good candidate **System** moves. Each commits the pawn to a special role, and we will examine the pros and cons of these moves later.

d) 5 ♗g5 again prematurely commits a piece to a square of dubious distinction.

e) The same is true of 5 ♗d3, which also leaves the d-pawn unprotected at a critical time.

f) 5 ♘ge2 could very well be a good move, but it must be premature to make it at this point before any other development decisions are taken. It could be that one wishes to play f4 followed by ♘f3 in the future, and ♘ge2 is too committal at this point.

g) 5 g3 is ridiculous because it commits the bishop to a dubious diagonal.

h) 5 h3 is ridiculous since it is a defensive move in a situation where there is no attack.

The 5 ♘f3 line

There are many who would argue with our cavalier dismissal of 5 ♘f3. It has probably been played more often in this position than any other move, so how can I dismiss it out of hand? The answer is simple. It is not a **System** move. It may be a perfectly good move that forces Black to play accurately to maintain equality; however, we are after more than equality. We want to pursue the **System** ideas to get an advantage.

After 5 ♘f3, play normally proceeds 5...0-0 6 ♗e2 e5! *(D)*.

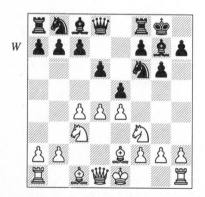

The fact that Black can get away with this move at such an early stage should make one suspicious of White's strategy. The point is that White cannot win a pawn by 7 dxe5 dxe5 8 ♕xd8 ♖xd8 9 ♘xe5 ♘xe4!, and if now 10 ♘xf7? then 10...♗xc3+ wins. Therefore, White usually continues more quietly with a move such as 7 0-0. Now, 7...♘c6 *(D)* already begins to pose serious threats to the white centre.

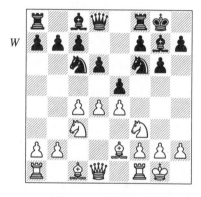

For example, Black threatens to play 8...exd4 9 ♘xd4 ♘xe4! 10 ♘xc6 ♘xc3 11 ♘xd8 ♘xd1, when he has won a pawn. This activity is very different from what Black achieves when he plays ...e5 in the 5 f3 line. Then the e4-pawn is well defended, and White need only concern himself with making sure d4 is also well protected.

The reader should familiarize himself with the above combination as this is the heart of how to play hypermodern defences. Because of this threat, White now usually plays either:

a) 8 d5 ♘e7, after which Black will, by playing ...♘e8, seize the initiative on the kingside with ...f5; or

b) 8 ♗e3, after which Black has little difficulty equalizing by 8...♘g4. The latter move points to one of the difficulties that White frequently faces: the queen's bishop belongs on e3 if he wishes to play to maintain his centre. However, Black can frequently counter with ...♘g4, putting pressure on d4 and threatening to exchange White's best minor piece.

The 5 f4 line

5 f4 was one of the historically first moves to be tried. This came in the days before the hypermodern ideas were very much understood, and appears to yield White a terrific centre which will sweep everything before it. But appearances are deceptive. In actuality, the move also weakens the e4-pawn, which can no longer be defended by a pawn. Thus, after the moves 5...c5 6 d5 (if 6 dxc5, then 6...♕a5 is good for Black) 6...0-0 7 ♘f3 e6 (D), Black will be able to open up the e-file to his advantage.

White's play above certainly seems consistent, and it took me a long time to decide between 5 f4 and 5 f3. The position after 7...e6 in the above line seems to offer White many

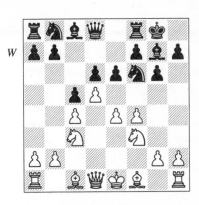

possibilities. The reader should convince himself that here 8 e5 dxe5 9 fxe5 ♘g4 only further increases White's difficulties. This line, and the lines derived from it, are very important. There is a major fight going on in the centre, and little things can make a big difference. If White can turn that fight to his advantage, then 5 f4 could be the correct way to proceed. However, the evidence as of today is that it is not possible for White to do this, and further, and possibly more importantly, 5 f4 leaves the centre over-extended, and one would expect a significant reaction by Black. The final word on this line has certainly not been said; however, we consider the move 5 f4 to be wrong (very subtly) because it over-exposes the white centre.

The 5 f3 line

In view of the coming challenge to White's centre by either ...c5 or ...e5,

White does best to prepare to hold his d4-pawn in place as long as possible. In order to do this, he must use the g1-knight and also the c1-bishop. The bishop must go to e3, which is the only place from which it can support d4. It must be able to rest securely there without having to worry about being exchanged by ...♘g4. So, we come to our **System** recommended move: 5 f3 *(D)*.

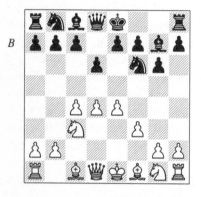

This move establishes firm control over e4, and prevents an eventual ...♘g4, thus paving the way for an early ♗e3 together with ♘ge2.

It would be rather euphoric to believe that all this comes clearly out of my present-day understanding of the **System**. However, in following all the arguments above, it should be clear that what fuels Black's counter-attack are the moves ...e5 and ...♘g4 after White has played ♗e3. This is strong motivation for eliminating the possibility of ...♘g4 and

preparing to defend the centre by ♗e3 and ♘ge2.

The above arguments are not typical **System** arguments. The fact that ...♘g4 is strong is something that is the result of tens of thousands of games and much discussion over the chess board in top tournament play over the past 50 years.

How should Black continue after 5 f3?

The 6...e5 line

Let us now look at how the **System** selects the moves that follow. One important continuation is 5...0-0 6 ♗e3 e5 7 ♘ge2 (it is necessary to be able to reply to ...exd4 with ♘xd4, as after ♗xd4, ...♘c6 would again threaten to exchange White's valuable bishop). The reader should note that the nature of the white pawn position has made his dark-squared bishop considerably more valuable than his light-squared one. Now follows 7...c6 8 ♕d2 *(D)*.

All of White's moves are a logical harmonious continuation of the plan begun with 5 f3.

From about 1952 until the 1980s, 8 ♕d2 had been considered bad. The reason was that Black can now make a break into the centre by means of 8...exd4 9 ♘xd4 d5 and threaten to isolate White's e-pawn. If White meets this by 10 cxd5 cxd5 11 e5 ♘e8 12 f4, Black's coming ...f6 will

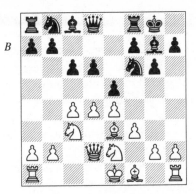

soon show that White's central set-up is weak. However, it was then discovered that White can play 10 exd5! cxd5 11 c5 ♘c6 12 ♗e2 ♖e8 13 0-0 with an excellent position.

Black also can continue less aggressively with 8...♘bd7 9 0-0-0 (the **Systematic** way to continue) 9...a6 10 ♔b1 b5 11 ♘c1 exd4 12 ♗xd4 leading to an excellent position for White.

So, the variation beginning with 6...e5 is again considered good for White, and Black has had to search for other means of defending against the 5 f3 variation.

The 6...♘c6 line

All lines where Black does not play 6...e5 consist of Black holding back his ...e5, and instead making some demonstration on the queenside first, mostly against the c4-pawn by means of ...b5. One very popular line of play after 5 f3 0-0 6 ♗e3 is 6...♘c6 (D).

This is a flexible move that can be a prelude to ...e5, or to ...a6 followed by ...♖b8 and ...b5. The move waits for White to choose his set-up, and then the c6-knight may be very useful. In the meantime, it avoids making a target by ...e5. However, the move threatens nothing, which is White's cue to action with Principle 9: **Attack or make a Space-Grab**. Well, we know that attacks that try to enforce h4-h5 in this position will not work as Black will open the centre by ...e5, long before the attack gets serious. But how about the space grab? Before Black gets in his ...b5, why can't White get in b4? This is undoubtedly the correct strategy, and another major contribution of this book.

After 7 ♖b1!! (D) Black has difficulty in finding a workable plan.

The move b4 is imminent and will sweep aside all of Black's hopes on the queenside once it is played. White need only be careful about his

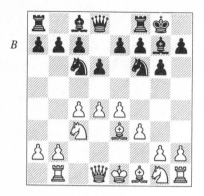

timing, as there may be tactical counter-chances starting with ...e5 and if d5, then ...♘d4. So we have:

a) On 7...♗d7 (7...a6 leads to similar play) White plays 8 b4. Now, in order to avoid being swept away, Black is practically forced to play 8...e5 9 d5 ♘d4 10 ♘ge2 ♘h5! 11 ♕d2! (11 ♘xd4 exd4 12 ♗xd4 ♕h4+ is too strong; however, now ♗f2 becomes possible as the c3-knight is defended). Now Black can no longer maintain the d4-knight without sacrificing a pawn in a rather unproductive way. If 11...♕f6, then 12 ♗g5. Or if 11...♕h4+ 12 ♗f2 ♕f6 13 ♘xd4 exd4 14 ♘e2. And 11...c5 12 dxc6 is hardly to be considered. So Black must play 11...♘xe2 12 ♗xe2, when White has an excellent position, several tempi ahead of similar positions that occur in this variation. 12...f5 can be met by 13 0-0, when 13...♘f4 14 ♗d1 ♕g5?! 15 ♔h1 ♕h5 16 ♗c2 gives White a formidable queenside initiative, while Black's

attack still has a long way to go before it becomes dangerous. Nor does 13...f4 14 ♗f2 ♗f6 15 ♕e1 g5 16 c5 offer Black much as White is again well ahead compared to usual positions in this variation.

b) Nor does 7...a5 8 a3! change anything. White will still advance b4, and not worry about the a-file, which will belong to White in the not-too-distant future.

c) On the immediate 7...e5 8 d5 ♘d4 (8...♘e7 9 b4 and the queenside attack is under way) 9 ♘ge2 c5 (if 9...♘xe2, 10 ♗xe2 and White is several tempi ahead of the standard variations in which White attacks on the queenside and Black on the kingside) 10 dxc6 ♘xc6 and White has a large positional advantage.

The Byrne Variation: 5...c6 6 ♗e3 a6 7 ♕d2 b5

For many years, I used to defend against the Sämisch Variation (5 f3) with the invention of the Byrne brothers, ...c6 and ...a6 intending ...b5. I can't recall ever losing a game with this line. In the Final of the 5th World Correspondence Championship, I played the following game:

H. de Carbonnel – H. Berliner
5th World Correspondence Ch,
1965-8

| 1 | d4 | ♘f6 |
| 2 | c4 | g6 |

3	♘c3	♗g7
4	e4	d6
5	f3	c6
6	♗e3	a6 *(D)*

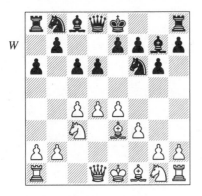

7	♕d2	b5
8	0-0-0	♕a5!
9	♔b1	♘bd7
10	g4	♖b8
11	h4	h5!
12	g5	♘h7
13	♖h2?	

White should play 13 f4. After this White played more passive moves, and eventually became the victim of a brilliancy[1]. However, Black's play appears to give him good prospects in any case. Therefore, there is good reason to question White's set-up in the above game. Up to move 6, everything is according to **The System**. However, at move 7, White should consider how to best meet the coming advance 7...b5.

One of the matters that faces White in the King's Indian, is that Black can choose a set-up that allows him to go to any of possibly 2 to 4 methods of counter-attacking the white centre. The bogey on White's back is how to play to be ready for all of these. It is very much like some openings we have already examined, in which White must establish move-pairs and be ready to respond to any of Black's counter-thrusts.

However, one aspect of all this is that one must be sure that a threat is really a threat. Here the coming 7...b5 opens several possibilities for Black. He could play ...bxc4, and after ♗xc4 play ...d5 and further weaken White's centre. He may also want to continue with ...b4 at some future time, and thereby get more space on the queenside. White must establish which of these threats is worthy of countering.

Consider the normal developing move 7 ♗d3, and the continuation 7...b5. This cannot be played for tactical reasons, because White will respond 8 e5! ♘fd7 9 f4 with a strong space advantage. Black does not have any meaningful breaks, e.g. 9...b4 10 ♘a4 ♕a5 11 ♘f3 c5 12 dxc5 ♘xc5 (12...dxe5 13 ♗e4!) 13 ♘xc5 dxc5 14 ♗e4 with a big advantage.

---

1   The game and notes are presented in Chapter 7 (Game 11).

So Black must play either 7...0-0 or 7...♘bd7 first. Since both these moves have to be played by Black in this variation, it does not appear to matter which is played first. Let's consider 7...0-0. White then continues his development with 8 ♘ge2 and now comes 8...b5 (D).

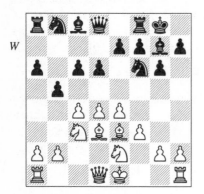

The Byrne Counter-Attack

This position has been examined thousands of times by well-qualified players all over the world. Is the black attack something worth preventing? Almost everyone seems to believe that is the case. But is it really? White can be happy about the fact that Black has had to make a concession by castling or moving the b8-knight in order execute his plans. But now on to the position at hand. How is White to meet the twin threats of ...bxc4 and a possible ...b4? The answer is the simple 9 cxb5!. If Black now plays the unthematic

9...cxb5, White has everything his own way. It is like certain positions from the Ruy Lopez. White has a very strong centre, and can operate anywhere on the board. So if this is to be a meaningful variation, Black must play 9...axb5, whereupon White plays his ace: 10 b4! (D).

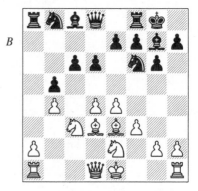

Now Black should play 10...♘bd7, but 11 a4! bxa4 12 ♖xa4 gives White a significant space advantage on the queenside and complete command of the centre. If seems safe to say that here Black has not realized any of the counter-attacking possibilities he was looking for when he went into this line.

What to do Versus the King's Indian

Have we mapped out a battle plan against the King's Indian that will carry you to victory in all future contests? Of course not! We have applied the **System** principles to what is most likely the right plan, but much is left incomplete. There are some things that I am quite sure of and which the reader sympathetic to my approach would be well advised to remember.

a) 5 f3 is definitely the right way to proceed. Anyone who believes he/she is pursuing Nirvana with 5 ♘f3 or 5 ♗e2 or any number of other alternatives may be learning some clever traps, but he/she will not be developing a long-term winning plan.

b) The basic plan for White, due to the lack of competition in the centre, is:

b1) Be sure the centre is secure by developing the bishop to e3 and knight to e2 when required.

b2) If Black fails to challenge with ...e5 then make a space-grab on the queenside with a well-timed b4 advance.

b3) If Black challenges the centre with ...e5, then control d4, and build up pressure on the d-file. This will eventually force Black to play ...exd4, after which White owns a significant part of the board.

b4) If Black challenges with ...c5, then play d5 and handle the position as if it were a Modern Benoni (see Chapter 6, p.119).

6 Miscellaneous Opening Analysis

In this chapter, we present analysis and example games on various opening variations. There are sections on:
  a) The Semi-Tarrasch Defence;
  b) The Tarrasch Defence;
  c) The Queen's Gambit Accepted;
  d) The Modern Benoni;
  e) The Benko Gambit.

The Semi-Tarrasch Defence

The Case Against the Semi-Tarrasch

In Chapter 4 we demonstrated strong advantages against all defences to the Exchange Variation of the QGD. That is, after 1 d4 d5 2 c4 e6 3 ♘c3 ♘f6 4 cxd5 exd5 5 ♗g5, Black seems to have interminable difficulties that we have found no way of overcoming. However, it is possible to play 4...♘xd5, and go into the Semi-Tarrasch Defence. This defence leaves White with a lead in development and complete control of the centre. It has always seemed to me to be rather lacking in concept

for Black. However, Black does exchange two minor pieces, which reduces White's attacking chances, and Black will get a queenside pawn majority for the ending, if he survives to get there.

An Unusual Departure

After Black's 4...♘xd5, White's best play is 5 e4 ♘xc3 6 bxc3 c5 7 ♘f3 (D).

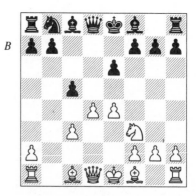

Clearly White has been playing all **System** moves. On his last move, he is allowed to block his f2-pawn since White already controls the whole centre, and the pawn is not needed to support it. The only deficit of 7 ♘f3 is that it allows Black to exchange another pair of pieces, thus reducing the advantage of controlling the centre. In the above position, Black usually continues 7...cxd4 8 cxd4 ♗b4+ 9 ♗d2 ♗xd2+ 10 ♕xd2 0-0 *(D)*.

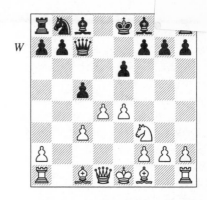

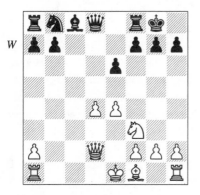

Then White (to move) has a development count of −4, and Black −5. So, White has a 1.5 tempi lead in development, and controls the whole centre. However, he must show what he can do with this. We consider this position below.

First, we dispose of an interesting sub-line played by Korchnoi, as it again shows how one should reason about applying **The System**. In the game Kupka-Korchnoi, Luhačovice 1969, Korchnoi played the unusual 7...♕c7 *(D)*, and it is this move that gives us an interesting chance to study the application of **The System**.

Black's last move can hardly be described as a developing move. Its sole purpose is to prevent the natural development of White's f1-bishop, since 8 ♗c4 cxd4 now forces 9 ♕xd4. Also, 8 ♗d3 is not playable since 8...cxd4 9 cxd4 ♕c3+ wins a piece. Now, clearly the most logical moves are 8 ♗d3 and 8 ♗c4, but after rechecking the above variations, we come to the conclusion that neither is playable.

What about 8 ♗e2? That is what was played in the above-quoted game, but it is a poor move since the bishop will have to move later to get a better post. This is like giving Black a free move. Nor are purely preventive moves such as 8 ♗d2 or 8 ♕b3, that are intended to keep the black queen out of c3, justified. Also 8 ♗b5+ ♗d7 9 ♗xd7+ ♘xd7 10 0-0 only aids Black's development. Remember the **System** principle that one does not make defensive moves during the opening, unless material has already been won, or they are part of normal development.

So what is the answer? Can the **System** survive such artificial attacks as 7...♕c7? Most certainly so; what about 8 ♖b1? This is, in a very real sense, a move that improves the position of one of White's pieces, and very importantly it side-steps the threat of ...♕c3+ with an attack on the rook. Now, if Black continues 8...♗e7, White can calmly play 9 ♗d3 as 9...cxd4 10 cxd4 ♕c3+ 11 ♔e2 will turn out very well for White. His king is in no real danger, while Black must lose time retreating his queen to safety.

A very instructive example, the moral of which is: "When you know you are in a **System** position, don't let your opponent bluff you into making an inferior move such as 8 ♗e2".

The Main Lines

However, the main line, to which we now return, is 7 ♘f3 cxd4 8 cxd4 ♗b4+ 9 ♗d2 ♗xd2+ 10 ♕xd2 0-0 *(diagram repeated here)*.

I have always wondered at the audacity of Black to play this position. His development count is −5, while White's (to move) is −4. Besides being 1.5 moves ahead in development, White has complete control of the centre. All Black has to show for this is the queenside pawn majority, which at this stage of things does not amount to much. However, we are

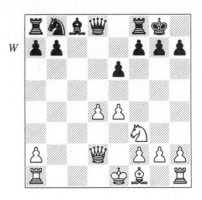

now faced with one of our regular **System** decisions which has a strong bearing on the value of this position: where is the f1-bishop to go? One of the popular moves is 11 ♗c4, which exerts strong influence on the centre. However, one should ponder the future of this bishop at c4. It can support an eventual d5, but that would lead after ...exd5 to either:

a) ♗xd5 with a strong bishop at d5 in a position of severely diminished material; or

b) exd5 with a passed pawn of doubtful value with so much material off the board.

The other alternative, 11 ♗d3, seems rather passive until one considers the pawn structure. With the indicated future e4-e5 advance, White will increase the scope of the bishop significantly and make it harmonious with the pawn structure, while signalling a possible attack on the black king. These facts make it clear that White should play 11 ♗d3 as the bishop is needed on the b1-h7 diagonal, where it cooperates beautifully with the white pawns on dark squares to control the centre.

Now Black has two usual lines of play: 11...♘c6 or 11...b6. In the first, Black plans to swap queens and go into an ending with a spatial inferiority, but hopes to capitalize on the backward d-pawn. In the second he plays the middlegame and hopes to keep White from working up a significant attack against the black king. I originally believed that White could keep a meaningful advantage against either line. Here was my analysis:

The 11...♘c6 Variation
11...♘c6 brings us to the following position *(D)*:

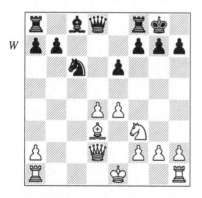

White replies 12 e5, the move that he planned when playing 11 ♗d3. Now play continues 12...♕a5 and the queens will be exchanged, after

which White has a minimal space advantage, which hardly seems enough to have real hopes of winning. I have won some correspondence games from this position, but in each case the defence was somewhat suspect. However, the real issue has always been the 11...b6 line.

The 11...b6 Line
After 11 ♗d3 b6 *(D)* we have a critical position.

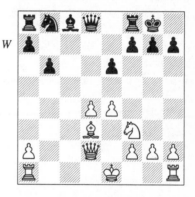

12 e5! ♗b7 13 ♘g5! (attack!) 13...h6 14 h4 and now:

a) 14...hxg5 15 hxg5 g6 (there is no other hope; 15...f5 16 gxf6 is hopeless, and 15...♖e8 16 ♕f4 ♘c6 17 ♗h7+ ♔f8 18 ♗g6 wins immediately) 16 ♕f4 ♔g7 17 ♕f6+ ♕xf6 18 gxf6+ ♔g8 19 ♖h2 ♗xg2 (on 19...♘c6, 20 ♔d2 threatens the unstoppable mate starting with ♖ah1) 20 ♖xg2 ♘c6 21 ♖h2 ♘xd4 22 ♖h3 and the mate is stoppable only by sacrificing the knight with 22...♘f3+.

Black can, of course, delay capturing the g5-knight, and we now look at this.

b) On 14...♗xg2! 15 ♖g1 ♗b7 (Black must not block the d-file with 15...♗d5, as after 16 ♘xe6! fxe6 17 ♕xh6 ♖f7 18 ♕h7+ ♔f8 19 ♗g6 ♕c7 20 ♖g3 ♘c6 21 ♖c1 Black is essentially helpless) 16 ♘f3!? ♔h8 (not, of course, 16...♗xf3 17 ♕xh6 with mate to come) 17 ♗c2 and now:

b1) 17...♗xf3 18 ♕d3 g6 19 ♕xf3 with a very strong attack for the pawn, for example 19...♘d7 20 ♕e3! ♔h7 (20...♔g7 21 h5 g5 22 f4; or 20...♕xh4 21 ♗e4!) 21 h5 ♖g8 22 ♖h1 ♕f8 23 hxg6+ fxg6 24 ♗b3 ♖e8 25 ♖c1 with an overwhelming attack.

b2) However, 17...f5!! 18 exf6 ♕xf6! 19 ♘e5 ♘c6! holds the defence and establishes a win for Black.

The above lines are very tactical, and I have spent hundreds of hours with my computer analysing them. At move 16 in line 'b', there are other possibilities than 16 ♘f3!?, such as 16 ♘xe6 fxe6 17 ♕xh6 but 17...♖f7 holds. And I have also examined 15 ♖h2, which will keep the g5-knight at its post for a long time.

To the best of my understanding, the attack beginning with 13 ♘g5 just barely fails; however, a more powerful computer could very well

justify the move, and there are many traps as well. In view of the above, and the fact that the 11...♘c6 line yields White only a tiny advantage, it may very well be that the correct **System** move is not 7 ♘f3, but instead 7 ♖b1, which prevents the exchange of bishops. This line has recently found favour in GM play.

The Tarrasch Defence

We now take up another example of White's opening play in following the principles of the **System**. I have always regarded the Tarrasch Defence as being a particularly weak opening for Black, but after the success that Spassky had with it (one win, four draws) in his 1966 world title match with Petrosian, maybe this view should be re-examined[1]. The opening starts with the moves 1 d4 d5 2 c4 e6 3 ♘c3 c5 *(D)*.

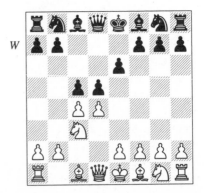

---

1   This section was written in 1967.

The reader will easily recognize White's first three moves as being **System** moves.

With his last move Black counter-attacks in the centre. White moves such as 4 ♘f3 are not adequate because of 4...cxd4, and White's centre is destroyed while Black's is still intact. Moves such as 4 e3 violate the **Option** principle by blocking in a bishop unnecessarily. So 4 cxd5 must be correct.

After Black replies with 4...exd5, his d5-pawn is forever in danger of becoming isolated and weak. Therefore, White adjusts his strategy; he can no longer dominate the centre, but instead prepares to take advantage of the weak black set-up there. Therefore, White plays 5 ♘f3, supporting the d-pawn so that ...cxd4 would not have to be met with ♕xd4, exposing the queen. Here, blocking the f-pawn is no longer important; the position is open and piece-play is required for centre control.

After Black replies 5...♘c6, White must decide how he is going to mobilize the remainder of his pieces. It seems premature to decide whether the c1-bishop is better placed at f4 or g5, and e3 is unthinkable. The only alternative plan is to fianchetto the f1-bishop along the long diagonal by first playing g3. Up to now in our discussions, we have never mentioned this idea, which stems from hypermodern practice. Indeed, since

System moves are dedicated to relentless pursuit of set objectives, this noncommittal form of development seldom fits in. Here, however the move helps to intensify the attack against the already weak d-pawn, and is therefore the correct plan. It is interesting to note that of the thousands of lines of **System** play that I have developed over the years, this is the only one in which this manoeuvre is used (it was first employed by the great Akiba Rubinstein in the early 1900s).

Play now continues 6 g3 ♘f6 7 ♗g2 ♗e7 8 0-0 0-0 9 ♗g5 *(D)*.

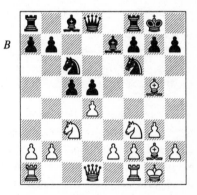

All these moves are natural and easy to understand. Now, we have arrived at a well-known 'book' position; one of the few times that 'book' and the **System** agree! This position has been generally regarded as favourable to White and so it is. But in the 1966 World Championship match, four games continued 9...cxd4 10

♘xd4 h6, and now each time Petrosian played 11 ♗e3. This move seems quite illogical, and is certainly not in accord with the principles of the **System**, as the earlier moves appear to be. It is clear that the bishop must move, and 11 ♗xf6 ♗xf6 leads to nothing for White as Black now has the initiative in the centre. But what about 11 ♗f4 *(D)*?

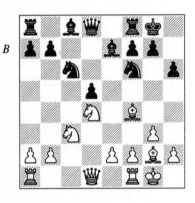

It is true that this is a retreating move; however, the retreat only comes after the bishop went to g5 to resolve the tension in the centre, and it succeeded at that. Also, the retreat is no time-loss, as Black's ...h6 is hardly a time-gain. So now, retreating is clearly better than exchanging. At f4, the bishop is very well placed, even helping to control the centre. Any attempt to dislodge it by ...♘h5 or ...g5 only weakens the black position. Now, in fact, White can continue with ♕a4 followed by ♖fd1 obtaining an overwhelming position.

I can find no real defence against this procedure. It would have been interesting to see what Spassky would have done against it.

The Queen's Gambit Accepted

I began playing 1 d4 d5 2 c4 dxc4 3 e4! *(D)* in the 1960s.

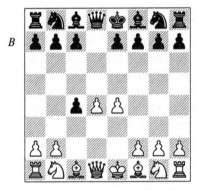

I had known for a long time that this was obviously the **System** move, but was intimidated by a general lack of confidence in the move among top players, and a lack of any analysis of my own to justify the move. However, when it became clear that in many variations White could allow Black to capture the d4-pawn with a pawn and not recapture, the basis for solid **System** play for White became apparent.

After 3 e4, Black can proceed in many ways. Among the standard moves are 3...e5 and 3...♘c6. Later, we take up an unlikely alternative: 3...b5?!. After 30+ years of advocating 3 e4, the world has now caught up with how to play the white side correctly, and we leave it to excellent opening books to document this.

Here, we want to show a few things that may not be generally known. The game below was played between David Bronstein and my computer Hitech. I had, of course, spent a great deal of time evolving private opening analysis for Hitech, and included among those lines was a lot about how to play the Queen's Gambit Accepted, its favourite line against 1 d4. Here we show one of the critical lines.

The 3...e5 line; David Bronstein Plays The System – up to a point

David Bronstein – *Hitech*
AEGON Man-Machine
Tournament 1990

1	d4	d5
2	c4	dxc4
3	e4!	e5
4	♘f3	exd4
5	♗xc4!	*(D)*

When it finally became clear (I attribute this mainly to Korchnoi) that White should not play 5 ♕xd4 or 5 ♘xd4 here, but should instead leave the d4-pawn alone to be a defensive burden for Black, then it was possible to find the correct way to play against the QGA.

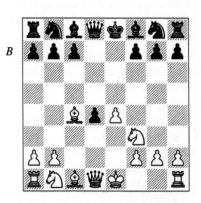

The strategy is akin to some things that Nimzowitsch tried against the French Defence. Leave a centre pawn to be taken by an opponent's pawn, and then let him worry about how to keep it (see Nimzowitsch's *My System*). Here the themes are a little different from those in the French, but the main point is that one does not put a piece on d4 to be attacked by Black, but instead just develops, ignoring the pawn deficit for a while.

5	...	♘c6!

After 5...♗b4+ 6 ♘bd2 ♘c6 7 0-0 Black is not as well off as in the present line.

6	0-0	♗e6!
7	♗xe6	fxe6
8	♕b3	♕d7
9	♕xb7	♖b8
10	♕a6	♘f6
11	♘bd2	♗b4! *(D)*

Play since the 5th move has been best for both sides, and is certainly in accordance with **System** principles. At first, when studying this line, I was reluctant to believe that 9 ♕xb7 could be a **System** move. However, there are several reasons for that:

a) It recaptures the pawn;

b) It creates weakness for Black on the c-file and elsewhere on the queenside;

c) The queen is not going to get chased around very much and is actually well placed.

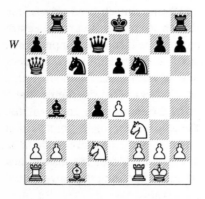

What is White's best move?

Black last move, 11...♗b4, is the invention of Hitech. It threatens 12...♗xd2, which leaves the white centre in bad shape. Hitech was not able to find the correct white reply, but together we found it. David Bronstein at the table was also not up to the task.

12 ♕d3?

This is an error, as the sequel shows. Correct is the imaginative 12 ♘c4 0-0 (on 12...♘xe4, 13 ♘fe5 ♘xe5 14 ♘xe5 ♖b6 {14...♕d6 15 ♘c6 ♖b6 16 ♕c8+ ♔f7 17 ♕xh8 ♕xc6 18 ♕xh7 wins} 15 ♕xa7 is too strong) 13 a3 ♗e7 14 ♖e1 ♖b3 15 ♗g5! with advantage. As can be seen, the light squares on the queenside are a headache for Black.

Now with the above error, the headaches switch to White, who has trouble guarding his e-pawn.

12 ...   ♗xd2!

13 ♘xd2   0-0!

Now Black's position is much freer, he is ahead in development, and his passed d-pawn is assuming threatening proportions. White's next move solves none of these problems.

14 a3   ♘e5

15 ♕g3 (D)

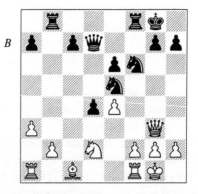

Apparently White expected to gain some time with this move, but he overlooked Black's reply, which is decisive.

| 15 | ... | ♘h5!! |

This is the end for White. If now 16 ♕xe5, 16...♖b5 wins the queen. So White must retreat and the knights start to bore into the position.

16	♕h4	♘f4
17	b4	♘e2+
18	♔h1	♘d3
19	♘b3	♕a4!
20	♘c5	

On 20 ♖b1, 20...♘c3 wins material, but now the back rank is vulnerable.

20	...	♘xf2+
21	♕xf2	♖xf2
22	♖e1	♕c2
23	♗g5	♘g3+
24	hxg3	♖xg2

0-1

An Ignored Move: 3...b5

In the older way of meeting the QGA, namely 3 ♘f3, Black's reply 3...b5 was quickly refuted. It had to do with the fact that White would play a4, e3 and get play on the h1-a8 diagonal and on the light squares in general. It also had to do with the fact that with the e-pawn on e3 it was not a target for counter-attack as it would be after 3 e4, and did not hinder activity on the h1-a8 diagonal.

With 3 e4, it is appropriate to ask if playing 3...b5 *(D)* might not work now.

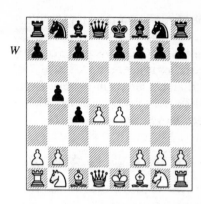

We would be surprised if it did, but it is worth investigating. After 3...b5, 4 a4 must be correct as it attacks Black's major weakness before he has time to consolidate, and also creates pressure to regain the sacrificed pawn. Black must reply 4...c6, whereupon it is **System** correct to play 5 axb5 cxb5 as this stabilizes the pawn structure prior to making any further development decisions.

Now, however, there are many possible paths for White, but again, it should be kept in mind that when there are several good developing moves, those that attack are to be preferred. Thus, it really comes down to whether 6 ♘a3 or 6 ♘c3 is best. One should look with a gimlet eye at 6 ♘a3 as this is not a normal square for the knight, and in this case only may have some merit because it cannot be met by 6...b4. However, in this set-up, White must be very careful about the weakness of his d4-pawn if and when Black gets to play ...♗b4+. There are many lines after 6 ♘a3 where this can happen, For instance: 6 ♘a3 ♗d7 7 b3 e5! and White is in trouble. Eventually, it becomes clear that White's best move must be 6 ♘c3 *(D)*.

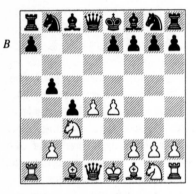

Now Black must find the best way to proceed. 6...♗a6 does not work because after 7 ♗f4 (threatening both ♗xb8 and ♘d5) there is no defence for Black. That the end should come so quickly bodes no good for Black. Also, 6...b4 7 ♘d5 e6 8 ♗xc4 exd5 9 ♗xd5 wins the rook in the corner.

So Black must pretty well play 6...♗d7. Now, the immediate 7 b3 b4 does not appear to work as there is no good way for White to continue. After 8 ♗xc4?! bxc3 9 ♗xf7+ (one should eschew such moves on general principles as this must be a premature attack) 9...♔xf7 10 ♕h5+ g6 11 ♕d5+ ♔g7 12 ♕xa8 ♗c6 13

♕xa7 ♗xe4 14 f3 ♘c6 Black stands considerably better.

I spent a long time here trying to understand what White has for his pawn. At the moment, it is only an advantage in space and development. Once Black plays ...e6, he will be fully in the battle. So maybe it would be good to increase the space advantage and prevent ...e6 by 7 d5! *(D)*, which also prevents the development of the black queenside.

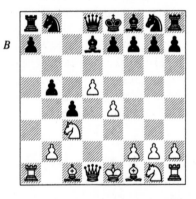

Now, if 7...e6 or 7...e5, White plays 8 dxe6 and Black has no good recapture. If 8...fxe6, 9 ♘xb5 ♗xb5 10 ♕h5+ gives White a great superiority, while 8...♗xe6 9 ♕xd8+ ♔xd8 10 ♘xb5 leaves Black sorry he ever undertook this defence. So Black must find another development plan, and this is not easy. 7...♘f6 8 e5 is unappetizing for Black. If all these normal moves are bad, then Black must be in deep trouble. Indeed, the best I have been able to find is 7...a5 8 ♘f3 and Black really has not much hope here, with ♘e5 in the wind and White having such a large space advantage.

The 3...♘c6 Line

The only other reasonable line besides 3...e5 is 3...♘c6. Now, the **System** move is clearly 4 ♘f3, which develops and defends the centre, whereas the only other reasonable move, 4 d5, would prematurely commit the white centre. According to the books, Black is now best advised to play 4...♗g4, which is answered simply by 5 ♗xc4. Now, Black dare not try to capture the d-pawn as f7 is too weak, so he must play 5...e6. Now, the threat against the d-pawn is real again, and White must decide how to proceed. It is easy to find 6 d5! *(D)*, which attacks the weak black queenside and forces some decisions on him.

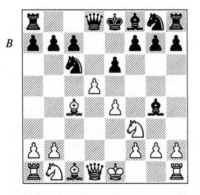

He cannot play 6...♘e5 because of 7 ♕a4+, nor can he play 6...♗xf3 7 ♕xf3 ♘e5 8 ♗b5+ c6 9 ♕c3 cxb5 10 ♕xe5 when White is, in effect, a pawn ahead.

So, Black must meet 6 d5 with 6...exd5 7 ♗xd5 and now White has many threats. He is much better developed, and is ready to attack while Black still has his kingside pieces at home. Best appears to be 7...♘f6 8 ♗xc6+ bxc6 9 ♕a4 with a strong game for White.

This is only a very sketchy treatment of this opening. The main lines follow 3...e5 and there are many defences. However, it is clear that White has a space advantage and easy development of his pieces, and this is definitely the right way to play against the QGA.

The Modern Benoni

The Benoni Defence was looked upon as something close to crazy in the 1920s and 1930s when it was first employed. It was felt that leaving White so much of the centre could not possibly be good. Black mostly was only interested in obtaining a draw, and would usually assume passive positions and eventually lose. The idea of Black playing ...e6 and ...exd5 was tried, but the mechanics of how to make it work were beyond the then practitioners of this defence.

Then in the late 1950s, Mikhail Tal showed what one could do with the black pieces. He would open the e-file for Black and aim his pieces at the white e4-pawn, and begin his counterattacks with any of ...c4, ...b5, or even ...♘g4. Black's play hinged mainly on the weakness of the e4-pawn, and the weaknesses that White made in defending it. Anyone who has followed **The System** up to here, knows that the premature ♘f3 leaves the e4-square in need of support, and the way the Modern Benoni was introduced was usually after White had already played this move, or White (not knowing or caring) would play ♘f3 at some time anyway. This, of course, meant that the e4-pawn would have to be defended by pieces that could be overloaded with other functions they should also fulfil. Below is an example of how White should play against the Modern Benoni.

H. Berliner – J. Rather
Eastern Open 1969

1	d4	♘f6
2	c4	c5
3	d5	e6
4	♘c3	exd5
5	cxd5	d6
6	e4	g6 (D)

The **System** approach to a defence such as the Modern Benoni is just to develop according to **System**

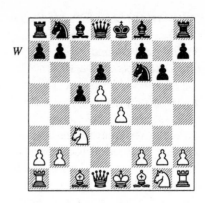

principles. So the above white moves are easy to understand. Now comes the first important **System** decision: Where should the f1-bishop go? It is possible to postpone this decision by playing ♘f3, and then deciding among e2, d3, and c4 for the bishop's location. However, this entails a certain neglect of the centre. In particular, the e4-pawn will be attacked by Black, and it would be easiest just to defend it and the light squares in that vicinity by f3. However, the commitment to f3 means that the g1-knight must go to e2, and this means that the f1-bishop must be developed first. The question is "To what square?".

The alert reader will notice that the above set-up resembles the recommended set-up against the King's Indian and also the Queen's Gambit Declined. This set-up is very solid since the knights mutually defend each other, which in this case is even more important as the g7-bishop will exert strong pressure on the long diagonal. So, if White wishes to play this set-up, he must continue with 7 ♗d3 right now. The only alternative, 7 ♗b5+ to exchange off his less good bishop, is premature in so far as the situation in the centre is still too fluid to make an exact determination of the worth of the minor pieces.

> 7 ♗d3 ♗g7
> 8 ♘ge2 0-0
> 9 0-0 *(D)*

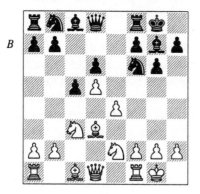

9 ... ♘a6

Black has the choice of this deployment of the knight or to play ...♘bd7 with an eye toward an eventual ...♘e5 and the exchange of the d3-bishop. However, 9...♘bd7 10 ♘g3 ♘e5 11 ♗e2 followed by f4, e5 and on ...dxe5 then f5 gives White a very strong attack that has basically put this line out of business. Details of this can be found in any good book on this opening.

10 f3 ♘c7

White's 10th move was far from standard in 1969 when this game was played. The reasons have already been given: solidity from which to build. White can now play ♗e3 when required and not have to worry about the reply ...♘g4. Now Black had to make another decision. 10...♘b4 does not work because of 11 ♗b1 and then a3 will drive the knight away. However, Black may just envisage the general advance of his queenside pawns. This could be better enforced with 10...♗d7 or 10...♖b8, supporting an eventual ...b5, and leaving open for the moment the question of where the a6-knight is bound.

11 ♗e3 ♖b8 *(D)*

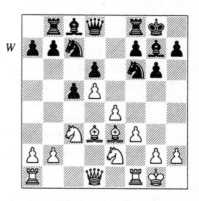

12 ♖b1!

This is the star move of this game. During the 1960s I had been analysing many of the **System** formations arising in various defences to 1 d4.

This frequently came up in connection with the World Correspondence Championship in which I was participating in at the time. One of the things that my understanding of **The System** did not include at the time was exactly what to do with rooks. The rules for the minor pieces were securely in place, but how and when does one utilize the rooks?

The conclusion that I came to is that in many of these openings when Black has created no direct object for attack, White should make a space-grab on the queenside with the move b4. This frequently has to be prepared, almost always by ♖b1, and never by a3 unless Black prevents b4 with ...a5. So this is a rook move with this purpose. Openings such as the Dutch Defence, Old Indian and King's Indian fall into this category.

In this case, there is actually much more to it. When one looks at the current position, one can see that White's game is beautiful, except he has been denied the use of the d4-square. If this could be occupied by a knight, then White's position would be overwhelming. So if White can play b4, a challenge to c5 would ensue. This could be reinforced by ♗e3 putting more pressure on the pawn. Black could attempt to meet this with an eventual ...b6 defending the c5-pawn sufficiently. However, in doing that, he would create a static formation on the queenside which White could attack in a number of ways. He could play for bxc5 and then depending upon how Black captures, play on the b-file or advance d6. Or he could play b5! and place a blockading piece on c4 from where it will stymie Black's position while White quietly prepares the advance e5. Contrary to these dynamic possibilities, a move such as 12 a4, which is frequently advocated by chess writers, represents a passive prevention of ...b5, and this leads to a passive position for White on the queenside.

Black could cautiously await events on the queenside, in which case White has clearly won the opening, or Black could just attempt to continue his queenside pawn advance. This is the way the game now continues.

| 12 | ... | b5 |
| 13 | b4! *(D)* | |

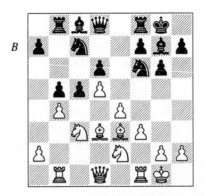

Now Black is faced with a threat to his b5-pawn after White plays bxc5. He has several choices:

a) 13...c4, which leaves his queenside pawns blocked and also gives up control over d4;

b) Defending passively by 13...a6 or 13...♗d7, when White will continue the attack on the queenside pawns and the squares they guard with a4; and

c) The game continuation. Black opts for freedom, but White's space advantage is too great.

13	...	cxb4
14	♖xb4	a5
15	♖b1	♗d7
16	♘d4	♕e8

The opening can now be appraised: White's pieces enjoy great freedom and are harmoniously placed, while Black is struggling to find meaningful scope for his.

17	♕d2	b4?

Black makes a bid for a place in the sun; however, it is ill-advised as he is behind in development, and the exchange of his good bishop on d7 will further weaken his position.

18	♘ce2	♘b5
19	♘xb5	♗xb5
20	♗xb5	♕xb5
21	♘d4 (D)	

Now White is assured of control of the c-file and play against the weak d6-pawn and queenside pawns. Black is now positionally lost because of his many weaknesses.

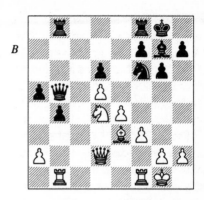

B

21	...	♕a4
22	♘c6	♖b7
23	♗d4	♖d7?

This loses a pawn. However, even after the better 23...♖a8, 24 ♖fc1 leaves White very much in command, as Black can undertake nothing.

24	♗b6!	♖a8
25	♗xa5!	

Black cannot now play 25...♖xa5 since 26 ♖xb4 ♕xa2 27 ♖b8+ ♗f8 28 ♕h6 leads to mate. So, he tries to save the situation by tactical trickery, which unfortunately for him does not work.

25	...	♘xe4
26	fxe4	♗c3
27	♖xb4!	♗xb4
28	♗xb4	♕xa2
29	♕d4	♖a4
30	♕f6	

Threatening ♗c3 with mates upcoming, and so winning more material.

30	...	♖xb4
31	♘xb4	♕c4

32	♖a1!	♛c8
33	♘c6	♛b7
34	h4	h5
35	♔h2	♔h7
36	♖a7	♛c8
37	♘e7	1-0

The idea of ♖b1 followed by b4 is present in all alternative defences. White will stabilize the centre when needed with f3, but basically continue his attack on c5 with the above plan. I can find no effective way to counter this except the idea already mentioned above, namely ...♘bd7. However, this line is never played any more because of the Penrose attack which yields a very strong white attack against the black kingside.

A typical line of play is 9...a6 10 a4 ♖e8 11 ♘g3 ♘bd7 12 f4 ♖b8 and now the break with e5, meeting ...dxe5 with f5, will leave Black helpless. The d5-pawn is very strong and there is the ever-present threat of fxg6 while White develops his pieces in the direction of Black's king. A possible continuation would be 13 e5 dxe5 14 f5 c4 15 ♗c2 b5 (15...♘c5 16 ♗g5) 16 axb5 axb5 17 ♘ce4 with a very strong attack well worth the pawn.

The Rather game, to me, epitomizes the way White should play. Black really never had a chance. I also wish to call the reader's attention to the **Response Pairs** present in this opening:

a) Black's ...♘bd7 should be met by f4 to keep the knight out of e5.

b) If the b8-knight decides to move to a6, then play will be against the queenside after f3, since f4 is no longer needed to keep the knight out of e5.

The Benko Gambit

Some Philosophy

As has been mentioned many times previously in this book, the management of pawns is of the utmost importance. No other piece contributes as much to the success of a position, because of the tyranny of the weak. The pawn is worth little and can therefore intimidate all pieces of greater value.

One issue that we have said little about is the capture of pawns by pawns. We have indicated that central pawns have a greater value than less central ones, and this leads to the age-old maxim of **Capture toward the Centre**. However, there are situations where this maxim does not apply and pawn-capture decisions must be made. It is those situations that are investigated in this section, and we aim to give firm rules for all situations.

Let us begin by looking at a very simple opening: 1 d4 ♘f6 2 c4 c5. Black offers a pawn sacrifice to get a pawn away from the centre. It is well known that after 3 dxc5, Black will regain his pawn and thus have achieved his goal of reducing White's majority in the centre. Thus, this offers White no hope of advantage. So, if White hopes to gain an advantage, he must play 3 d5. Now, it is possible to continue in many ways, most of which are taken up in this book. However, here we wish to see what we can learn from how to proceed against 3...b5?! *(D)*.

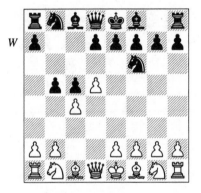

There are a number of things that should be immediately clear. Black again wishes to lure a more central pawn away by a capture of a less central one. How should White proceed? If he plays 4 b3 and stabilizes the pawn situation, he makes a totally uncalled-for defensive move and compromises his position at this early stage. If he lets Black capture on c4, White will be able to recapture the pawn with a piece, but he will have allowed Black to achieve

the goal of swapping the b-pawn for the c-pawn. There may be some merit to this for White, as he will gain somewhat in time.

One possibility is 4 f3 bxc4 5 e4 e6 6 ♗xc4 exd5 and Black has no real difficulties ahead. Also possible is 4 e3, which is clearly not a **System** move as it gives up on an early e4. Many other moves, such as 4 ♕c2, 4 ♘f3, 4 ♘d2, and 4 a4, have been played here, but the essence of all these attempts is that Black will capture on c4 and thereafter be able to operate effectively against the white centre and on the b-file. So how is White to play?

One thing that affects all these decisions is the discovery in the 1960s that if White plays 4 cxb5, Black can satisfactorily offer the permanent pawn sacrifice 4...a6!.

If this is met by 5 bxa6, Black gets a fine game on the queenside with play against the white pawns there, and on the half-open a- & b-files. Is there anything else that should be considered here?

The System Approach to the Benko Gambit

It took me a long time to understand that 4 cxb5 could be a **System** move. It captures away from the centre, but there is a critical difference: after 2...c5 White can avoid the capture by **advancing**; here he cannot. No matter how White plays, his c-pawn will be exchanged for the black b-pawn unless he plays the horrible 4 b3?. So, if this exchange is inevitable, why not make Black pay in some way? The most obvious and correct way is to capture: 4 cxb5!. Now, however, after 4...a6!, we should not be anxious to play 5 bxa6, but instead consider whether there is some positional advantage that can be gained while Black is recovering his pawn.

The principal advantage that is available is control of the centre. White cannot do this by 5 ♘c3 as after 5...axb5 he still cannot play 6 e4 b4, and the alternative of 6 ♘xb5 is not appealing at all. However, there is a way of taking the centre that we have seen again and again in **System** play. It is 5 f3! *(D)*.

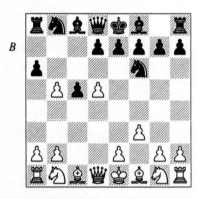

The 5 f3 line

Now it is Black who has a problem. 6 e4 cannot be prevented and it is

Black's decision as to whether he wants to recover the pawn now, or challenge the centre by ...e6. 5...e6 6 e4 exd5 7 exd5 ♕e7+?! 8 ♔f2! c4 9 ♘c3 axb5 (9...♕b4 10 ♕e2+ ♔d8 11 ♕xc4 ♗c5+ 12 ♔g3! ♗d6+ 13 ♔h3 leaves White two pawns ahead; his king is not really in much danger) is a line that has been played in top-level competition during 1997. Now White can play the excellent 10 d6! *(D)*.

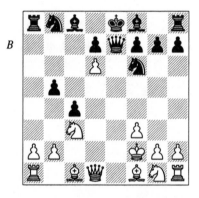

Then 10...♕xd6 11 ♕xd6 ♗xd6 12 ♘xb5 ♗c5+ 13 ♗e3 ♗xe3+ 14 ♔xe3 is winning for White. A much better line for Black is 10...♕e5! 11 ♕e2! ♕xe2+ (11...♗xd6 12 ♘xb5) 12 ♘gxe2 ♗xd6 13 ♘xb5 ♗c5+ 14 ♗e3 ♗xe3+ 15 ♔xe3 ♔e7! 16 ♘ed4! d5 17 ♗e2 ♗d7 18 b3 ♗xb5 (18...cxb3 19 axb3 ♘c6 20 ♘xc6+ ♗xc6 21 ♔d4 with a strong endgame advantage because of the outside passed pawn and the better bishop) 19 ♘xb5 cxb3 20 axb3 ♘c6

21 ♘d4! ♘xd4 22 ♔xd4 with a clear advantage. It should be noted that White's play in this line begins by disrupting Black's attempts to attack. 10 d6 splits the black forces, and after the tactics that follow, Black has exchanged his good bishop, and is left with weak central pawns that are on the same colour as his remaining bishop. White then proceeds to exchange the c-pawn, leaving him with an outside passed pawn in a very strong position.

The 5...axb5 line

If the aggressive 5...e6 fails, as it apparently does, then Black has nothing better than 5...axb5 6 e4 ♕a5+ (Black dare not play 6...b4, 6...♗a6 or 6...♕b6 as the reply 7 e5 is too strong) with the following position (D).

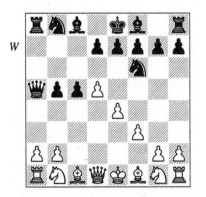

This sets before White an interesting problem. It appears as if there must be some easy way to refute this premature check. There are many possibilities: 7 ♗d2, 7 ♘c3, and even 7 b4?!. After having invested quite a bit of time studying these alternatives, it became clear that 7 ♗d2 b4 8 ♘a3 d6 9 ♘c4 ♕d8 (D) is very good for White.

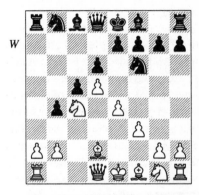

Black appears ready to put serious pressure on the d5-pawn, and White must be able to meet this without making any important concessions, such as giving up more of the centre. From a **System** point of view, he could continue with either 10 a4 or 10 a3 and have the advantage on the queenside. However, his centre has become weak as his d5-pawn is not supported by the queen and cannot be easily supported in the future by pawns or pieces. So Black can soon play ...e6, and thereafter will be able to wage a reasonable fight for the centre and the future of the game.

White must strike now on the queenside, before Black completes his development. He has the choice of 10 a3 or 10 a4. 10 a4 is a good positional move, but immediate action on the queenside is required. After 10 a4 e6 11 ♘e3! exd5 12 exd5 ♗e7 13 ♗b5+ ♘bd7! 14 ♘e2 0-0 15 0-0 ♗b7 Black has sufficient play against the d5-pawn to assure equality.

After the correct 10 a3, it is clear that for Black to play 10...bxa3 is a mistake because of 11 ♖xa3 ♖xa3 12 bxa3 and now White has a passed a-pawn and a great deal of room to support its advance as both bishops can now roam freely on the queenside. Examination of the passed-pawn situation shows that White's a-pawn is stronger than Black's protected passed pawn, since the a-pawn's advance is easily supported by pieces while the c-pawn's is not.

So, 10...e6, with the idea of challenging the centre, must be correct. Now, White must play a move that I am not at all sure is a **System** move. It is 11 ♘e3! *(D)*.

It moves a well-placed piece a third time; however, in the process it makes the deployment of White's kingside forces much easier. Also, the transgression is not that bad, as Black has moved his queen twice and arrived back at its original square. The development situation is actually quite well balanced: White's tempo count is −4 since his a1-rook is essentially developed, and Black's

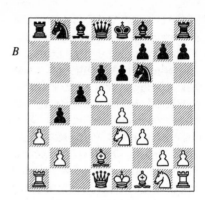

is −5 as his c8-bishop is essentially developed. Computer analysis likes 11 ♘e3, and it could well be the key move to this whole variation.

The important point is that, if White can maintain the d5-pawn, he will have split the black forces into two camps and they will not be able to coordinate on anything offensive, while White can operate on both wings. Black must now apparently acquiesce to 11...bxa3 12 ♖xa3 ♖xa3 13 bxa3 exd5 14 exd5, whereafter White can easily develop his kingside while Black struggles to find meaningful locations for his pieces. A possible continuation is 14...♗e7 15 ♗b5+ ♘bd7 16 ♘e2, with an excellent position for White.

I do not believe there is any merit in the sacrificial line 11...♗e7?!, which is met simply by 12 axb4 ♖xa1 13 ♕xa1 exd5 14 exd5, when Black has very little to show for his pawn minus. The e3-knight in this very unusual post holds everything together nicely, and White now has a wonderful position besides his extra pawn.

Clearly, this whole variation needs some testing, as I believe it is completely new, having originated with this book. The theme of 11 ♘e3! is to maintain the d5-pawn until reinforcements arrive in the best style of Western movies. It turns out that Black just cannot attack the d5-pawn more times than it can be defended, and when the pawn survives, it destroys Black's ability to operate. The fact that variations in this section are very different from any encountered anywhere else in this book does not mean that they are not **System Correct**. 11 ♘e3! is a very surprising move, but it has excellent effects, and it only gives up a unit of time that had already been gained chasing the black queen.

Once having come to the realization that White's 4 cxb5 is a correct **System** move, the first few moves in these lines against the Benko Gambit are not difficult to understand.

However, the play beyond that is very complicated, involving ideas that have not been invoked in any other parts of this book. However, as everywhere in this book, the centre is paramount, and the impeding of the opponent's development by controlling the centre is the main theme. Many of these lines are completely new, and have come into being as the result of examining current (1998) opening theory and dabbling with my friend Fritz 5.0 to see where inadequacies in White's play can be overcome. Clearly, in an enterprise such as this, there will be mistakes. However, I have spent a great deal of time and effort to find the right way, and the analysis above, while not fully complete, appears to be it. The nature of the play is such that, while there may still be room for improvement for Black, it is not a very inviting position to play, and there is probably at least one improvement for White for every one for Black. There will be few players who will want to test these variations as Black.

7 Illustrative Games

The System On Offence

In this chapter, we present some examples of how to play **The System** perfectly. Each game is annotated to show the tactical and positional issues, and to discuss the **System** decisions that come up at critical points. These decisions again show:

a) How the initiative is maintained;

b) How options are conserved while developing smoothly; and

c) How board control works.

Game 1

H. Berliner – G. Hunnex

US Open Ch 1955

This was my first **System** game. Every move was clear and best. And everything followed from one move to the next. I still remember the elation I felt at the whole experience.

1	d4	d5
2	c4	e6
3	♘c3	c5
4	cxd5	exd5
5	♘f3	♘c6
6	g3	c4 (D)

Our approach to the Tarrasch Defence is discussed in Chapter 6,

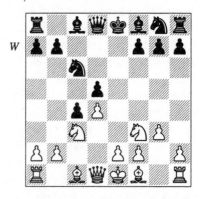

p.112. Black's last move is the Swedish Variation, which was in fashion at the time. It is not to be recommended, since 6...c4 releases the tension against the white centre, and thus makes it easier for him to proceed.

| 7 | ♗g2 | ♗b4 |
| 8 | 0-0 | ♗xc3 |

This is a senseless pursuit of some tactics to threaten to win a pawn. It gives up Black's best piece, and solidifies the white position. White has completed the development of his minor pieces, and Black should do likewise by 8...♘ge7. The c3-knight was not going anywhere yet, so Black should have retained for as long as possible the option of capturing it.

| 9 | bxc3 | ♕a5 (D) |

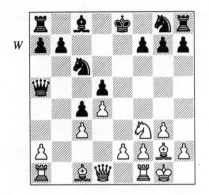

Up to here, White's **System** moves have been easy to find. Now, however, he must deal with the threat to the c3-pawn. Is that a real threat? If so, how should he defend? What should White's general plan be to utilize his lead in development? For instance, 10 ♗d2 appears to be a plausible move, and after 10...♘f6 11 ♘e5 White certainly stands a little better. But is that the right way to play the position? Certainly, the idea of defending the attack on an obscure pawn is hardly in line with **System** play. If you examine the position, you will see that the move 10 e4 gives White's pieces many new opportunities, and is also part of a direct attack on Black's centre. How can this move be prepared? Can it be played now? To answer the last question correctly, you will have to do some accurate analysis of the tactics in the position. However, that is typical of correct **System** play. If you want to take advantage of what

is in a position, then you have to be ready to utilize the tactical potential that is there. Given the first move, the God of Tactics is ever ready to smile on White.

Here, if we consider 10 e4, we must look at both replies 10...dxe4 and 10...♕xc3. Thus, 10 e4 ♕xc3 11 exd5 ♕xa1 12 dxc6 leaves Black in a helpless state in view of his king in the centre and his lack of development. The other alternative is the game continuation.

| 10 | e4! | dxe4 |
| 11 | ♘g5 | ♘f6 |

If Black were to defend his pawn with 11...f5, then 12 d5 ♘d8 13 ♕d4 would be much too strong. Since Black's king is in great danger, he must look to castle quickly.

| 12 | ♘xe4 | ♘xe4 |
| 13 | ♗xe4 | 0-0 (D) |

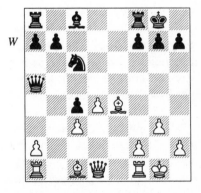

Now, White is again faced with a number of minor threats and must decide how to continue. He has the two bishops, which in an open position like the present are formidable. He also is better off in the centre, and has a minor edge in development. If he now plays 14 ♕c2 f5 15 ♗g2 ♗e6 16 ♖b1 ♗d5 Black is over the hump (the b7-pawn is defended as 17 ♖xb7 ♗xg2 18 ♔xg2 ♕d5+ followed by ...♘xd4 is fine for Black).

After some examination, it becomes clear White should deploy his rooks, and it can be observed that 14 ♖b1 serves to restrain Black's development by attacking the b7-pawn. But what about the two white pawns that are *en prise*? Again, intuition should tell one that these minor threats are of little import. If 14...♕xa2, 15 ♕h5 f5 16 ♗d5+ ♔h8 17 ♗f7!! ♕xb1 18 ♗g6 h6 19 ♗xh6 wins. And 14...♕xc3 15 ♗b2 ♕a5 16 d5 likewise leads to an overwhelming attack. The student should note in these variations that White must be ready and willing to trade advantages (material for attack). Otherwise, if he believes he must defend, he may soon end up with a passive position.

14 ♖b1!   ♗h3
15 ♖e1   f5

White must decide where to retreat the bishop. He must choose between the two diagonals, and here it is evident that the pressure against the queenside is White's most important asset, so the bishop should remain on the long diagonal. And ♗h1 is preferable to ♗f3 as the latter blocks the queen's mobility. The thought that the bishop is less developed at h1 than at f3 would be a typical classical chess thinking error. Just like a c8-bishop can be very useful in King's Indian-type positions, so the h1-bishop is placed as well here on the diagonal as anywhere else. No thought should be given to ♗xc6, which would actually give Black the better game because of the weak light squares surrounding White's king.

16 ♗h1!   ♖ae8 *(D)*

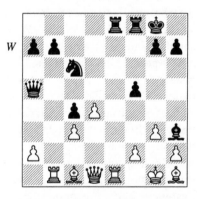

The game is now at its climax. Every piece for each side is developed. Who is winning? Even though all of White's pieces are on the first rank, he has a completely won game, because they are all extremely well positioned and cooperating beautifully.

White would like to play 17 ♖xb7, but then Black can play 17...♘xd4, right? No!! Remember, both sides can indulge in tactical tricks, and, as we have mentioned before, they favour White in **System** positions because he has maintained the advantage of the first move.

So let us look at that variation again. If 17 ♖xb7 ♘xd4 how about 18 ♖xg7+! then? 18...♔xg7 is met by 19 ♕xd4+ (the point is that the knight is now taken with check) 19...♔g6 20 ♖xe8 ♖xe8 21 ♕d6+ ♔g7 22 ♗h6+ ♔g8 23 ♗d5+ ♔h8 24 ♕f6#. On 18...♔h8, 19 ♖xh7+ ♔xh7 20 ♕h5+ (it is helpful that the h1-bishop is not in the way) 20...♔g8 21 ♕g6+ ♔h8 22 ♖xe8 wins. There are of course other lines, but the general scheme should be clear. It would be instructive to work out all the variations.

17 ♖xb7!! ♕xc3

Seeing the problem, Black plays the worse ...♕xc3, and loses the c6-knight.

**18 ♗d2 ♕xd4
19 ♗xc6 c3
20 ♗xe8 ♕d5**

If 20...cxd2 then would have come 21 ♗f7+ ♔h8 (21...♖xf7 22 ♖e8+ ♖f8 23 ♕b3+) and White is a rook ahead with an easy win.

21 ♖xg7+! 1-0

Black can neither capture the rook nor refuse, so he resigned. A game with a thrust to it that carries from opening to mating attack. Black's play was hardly the best, but it was certainly a **System** attack.

The next game is an excellent example of **System** play against a grandmaster. It involves rebuffing an attempt to seize the initiative at an early stage, and by means of a pawn sacrifice taking control of the whole position, so Black can hardly move and has many weaknesses.

Game 2
H. Berliner – A. Bisguier
*US Invitational Ch,
New York 1960*

1	d4	♘f6
2	c4	e6
3	♘c3	♗b4
4	♗g5	d5
5	cxd5	exd5

We are still not sure what the correct **System** 4th move against the Nimzo-Indian Defence is, but here 4 ♗g5 was played. "So how can this be a **System** game?" you ask. Well, hang on a minute, we have transposed into a known **System** position! It is easy to confirm that the position after Black's 5th move is a **System** position that could have arisen from the Queen's Gambit, as follows: 1 d4 d5 2 c4 e6 3 ♘c3 ♘f6 4 cxd5 exd5 5 ♗g5 ♗b4. Here 5...♗b4 is an ill-advised attempt to snatch the initiative from White.

6 e3

6 e3 is clearly the right **System** move as the place for the g1-knight cannot yet be determined. No thought

should be given to 6 ♕a4+ ♘c6, which only serves to displace the white queen.

    6 ...   **c5** *(D)*

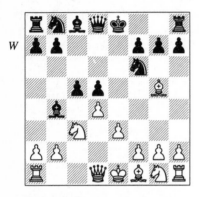

We are now at the main crisis of the game.

White has two basic choices for continuing his development: 7 ♘f3 or 7 ♗d3. After 7 ♘f3 h6 8 ♗h4 (8 ♗xf6 ♕xf6 is fine for Black) 8...g5 9 ♗g3 ♘e4 White has some discomfort in defending his knight, and Black seems to have achieved at least equality. On the other hand, 7 ♗d3 c4 8 ♗c2 ♕a5 9 ♘e2 ♘e4 10 ♗xe4 dxe4, and again Black is very well off. At this point one must ask oneself "What am I missing? Black cannot possibly get such a good position that quickly". Somehow 7 ♗d3 seems like the better move since it still allows the g1-knight to go to either e2 or f3, so let us look at that first. The real problem with the line given above is that 9...♘e4 is

strong. What can be done about that? After 9 ♗xf6, we would lose a pawn to 9...♗xc3+ 10 bxc3 ♕xc3+. Is that very bad?

This is the kind of examination and reasoning that one must do in trying to find the right move. It was exactly my train of thought as I played the game. There seems to be some basis for compensation for White. After the forced 11 ♔f1 (11 ♔f1 is better than 11 ♔e2 since now the g1-knight can come out with tempo by attacking the queen) 11...gxf6, Black has doubled isolated f-pawns, and his queen is out of play. Further, Black's king will have trouble finding a secure home. Well, is White's king not displaced too? Not so; it has a fine home on the kingside, although he will have some trouble getting his king's rook out. To elaborate the ideas in this line of play, and evaluate the various resulting positions before deciding to play 7 ♗d3, took me over 20 minutes. In this, I was aided by one of the **System** principles that says "Don't be afraid to sacrifice a pawn or two if this is needed to promote **System** strategic ends".

Now, Black continued with his strategy which in this case involved winning a pawn. Without too much consideration, he played the line we are expecting.

    7 ♗d3   **c4**
    8 ♗c2   **♕a5** *(D)*

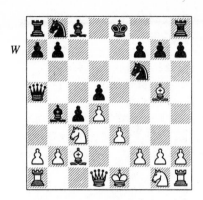

It is time for White to play his combination.

9	♗xf6!	♗xc3+
10	bxc3	♕xc3+
11	♔f1	gxf6
12	♘e2	♕a5
13	♘f4	

White puts his knight on a very strong post from which it can observe the weak d-pawn and threaten incursions such as ♘h5, if such prove opportune.

13 ...   ♘c6

This is the position that White evaluated when he played 7 ♗d3, and he decided that despite the pawn minus, White has the better game. Black has great difficulties in developing his pieces to active squares.

White must now decide how to develop his remaining forces. 14 ♕h5 is not good since 14...♕c3 causes White some embarrassment. Moves such as 14 g3 followed by ♔g2 are not aggressive enough. However, the time is ripe to develop the a1-rook.

14 ♖b1! *(D)*

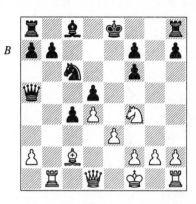

This move is correct and powerful since it ties the black bishop to the defence of b-pawn for the moment. Black is now faced with powerful threats such as e4, which would open up the centre while the king still has no safe haven. In view of this, Black decided to give back the pawn in order to mobilize rapidly.

14 ...   ♗d7

Black cannot play 14...♕xa2, since he would lose the d5-pawn.

15 ♖xb7   0-0-0

Now we must reappraise the position. Material is even; however, Black has a very bad pawn structure and a bad bishop, so all endgames must be lost for him. On the other hand, White must get his h1-rook developed, and be careful that the passed c-pawn does not become dangerous. Black's best chance is to seize the b-file, and White must prevent this. So White plays 16 ♕b1 to keep the

king confined, and Black answers
16...♕a6 to try to free him.

16	♕b1	♕a6
17	♖b5	♘e7
18	♖c5+	♗c6 (D)

Now it is safe to bring out the king
and put the rook on the b-file.

21	...	♖b7
22	♖b1	♕c7
23	♕a6 (D)	

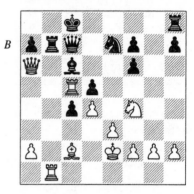

White must now hurry to neutral-
ize the b-file before Black can play
...♔c7 and ...♖b8.

19 ♕b4

No thought should be given to 19
♗xh7, which gives Black respite in
the face of much danger.

19...♕xa2 does not worry White,
as 20 ♗f5+ ♘xf5 (20...♔c7 21 ♖a5
wins) 21 ♖xc6+ ♔d7 22 ♕b7+ ♔e8
23 ♖xf6 gives him a mating attack.

19 ... ♕b6

This is a mistake after which Black
is lost by force. It would have been
better to play 19...♖d7 but White's
positional advantage is very great
and would gradually be brought to
bear. But now he has a quicker way.

20	♕a3	♖d7
21	♔e2!	

With this last move White's pieces
reach their peak efficiency and the
dual threats of ♘xd5 and ♗a4 are
impossible to answer. For instance
23...♖d8 24 ♗a4 ♔b8 (after 24...♖d6,
25 ♗xc6 wins a pawn) 25 ♖xb7+
♕xb7 26 ♖xc6 wins.

23	...	♔b8
24	♘xd5!	♘xd5
25	♖xc6	♖xb1

If he tries 25...♕d7 then 26 ♖xb7+
♕xb7 27 ♕xb7+ ♔xb7 28 ♖xc4,
and it is safe to resign.

26	♖xc7	♘xc7
27	♕xf6	1-0

Black must lose another rook.

What principles for middlegame
play can we develop from this example?

a) Clearly, tactical issues are the most important. If some set of moves seem desirable, look for some tactical means of accomplishing this. In this connection, note White's 7th, 9th, 14th, 19th moves, all of which seem to offer material without Black really being in a position to capitalize on it.

b) White's play seems to have a forward flow to it. There are no retreats unless a major advantage (sufficient to win) has first been attained. Instead, the pieces continue to improve their positions with each move, with the general effect that Black is forced to give ground. This effect can be better observed in less tactical games, but can be seen here from the first move on.

c) White's game never suffers from any organic defects, except in return for a winning advantage. This is very important; note for instance that White always has a sound pawn structure and maintains the better bishop. Giving up castling is not an organic defect as long as it does not result in a permanent problem for the king and rook.

Game 3
A. Alekhine – M. Euwe
World Ch match (game 6), Haarlem 1937

As mentioned in the Introduction, early in my career I was struck by the way Alekhine brought tremendous energy into his openings with White. I believe he was very close to discovering **The System** in the years starting with 1929.

In looking over these games now, I am struck with one example and his notes, which are given below, and could easily have been written by some early practitioner of **The System** (see Alekhine's *My Best Games of Chess 1924-1937*, p. 228). I have appended a few comments which are shown in square brackets.

1	d4	d5
2	c4	c6
3	♘c3	

"In my opinion this move gives White more chances of obtaining an opening advantage, and for the following reasons:

a) The dangers of the continuation 3...dxc4 in conjunction with 4...e5 are clearly shown in the present game;

b) The Winawer Counter-attack, 3...e5, can be met in a simple and effective manner by 4 cxd5 cxd5 5 e4! and if 5...dxe4, then 6 ♗b5+ ±;

c) In answer to 3...♘f6 4 e3 g6 I suggest 5 f3, which after 5...♗g7 6 e4 dxe4 7 fxe4 e5 8 d5 0-0 9 ♘f3 leads to a rather complicated position, still positionally favourable to White."

[Wow! Written in 1937 and very close to the mark.]

3	...	dxc4

4 e4! *(D)*

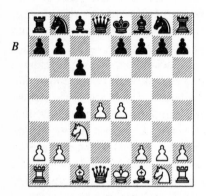

"It is almost incredible that this quite natural move has not been considered by the so-called theoreticians. White obtains now an appreciable advantage in development, no matter what Black replies." [Yeah, verily!]

4 ...   e5

"The alternative is 4...b5 5 a4 e5 (or 5...b4 6 ♘a2 ♘f6 7 e5 ♘d5 8 ♗xc4 ± [I do not agree with this evaluation – '=' is closer to the mark; the **System** way is probably 7 f3! e5 8 ♗xc4! ♕xd4 9 ♕xd4 exd4 10 ♘e2 ♗c5, but I have yet to find the killer here; this is one reason why the Slav is not included among openings being presented]) 6 axb5 exd4 7 ♗xc4! ♗b4! 8 ♖a4 a5 9 bxa6 and White will emerge a pawn to the good."

5 ♗xc4

"This sacrificial combination is certainly very tempting and, especially over the board, extremely difficult to refute; but it is by no means the necessary consequence of White's previous move, which has a value absolutely independent of the correctness of the piece sacrifice. The *positional* exploitation of White's advantage in space consists in 5 ♘f3! exd4 6 ♕xd4 ♕xd4 7 ♘xd4, after which Black would only get into trouble by trying to protect the gambit-pawn – for instance, 7...b5 8 a4 b4 9 ♘d1 ♗a6 10 ♗e3 ♘f6 11 f3 followed by ♖c1 and ♗xc4 with a clear positional advantage."

5 ...   exd4
6 ♘f3   b5?
[a blunder that loses]
7 ♘xb5!
and White won.

This game fragment and notes are most revealing. Alekhine clearly understood a lot of what **The System** is about. However, he knew he was flying in the face of convention, and even when he had it right, he could not control his sacrificial urge (5 ♗xc4? when the simple 5 ♘f3 would leave Black struggling to get breathing room).

The next game is a good illustration of the accumulation of the various positional advantages discussed in Chapter 1. In particular it is worthwhile to pay attention to the relative values of the pieces for Black and White. In the final position,

White's queen and rook essentially beat queen, rook and bishop.

Game 4
H. Berliner – S. Nyman
*5th World Correspondence Ch
Final, 1965-8*

1	**d4**	♘f6
2	**c4**	**c5**
3	**d5**	**e5**
4	♘**c3**	**d6**
5	**e4**	**g6** *(D)*

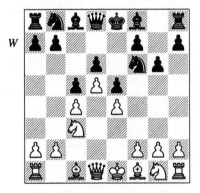

So far, clearly all **System** moves, but what now? We need to develop the rest of the minor pieces, but what goes where? In this kind of position, White can attack on the queenside with an eventual b4, or on the kingside with h4-h5, or he can attempt to do both. In this, one needs flexibility for the kingside pawn advance, which means the g1-knight should go to e2. The best location for the c1-bishop is still not clear. However,

based on the above, it is clear where the f1-bishop must go, and it must go there now!

6	♗**d3**	♗**g7**
7	♘**ge2**	**0-0**
8	**f3**	

Is this a **System** move? I think so! The problem is that there is so little pressure on White that he does not have to do anything other than build his position so as to keep his options open. Here, White would like to proceed with g4, ♘g3, h4-h5, with a very strong attack. So 8 f3 is a necessary precursor for this advance. We realize that we have nothing in this book about how to proceed in positions such as this. However, **System** principles do certify the c1-bishop as developed, and the king on e1 is not in need of shelter, so the opening is basically over, and it is time to proceed to the attack.

8	...	♘**a6** *(D)*

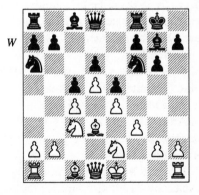

9 h4

Here I believe 9 g4 is better, and
if 9...h5?!, 10 h3! ♘h7! (10...h4 11
♗g5) 11 ♗e3 and now Black must
decide if he will venture 11...f5 or
perish inactively.

    9 ...   ♘c7

Now it is difficult to continue the
kingside attack correctly, since 10
g4 is met by 10...h5! 11 gxh5 ♘xh5
and Black has managed to cope.

    10 ♗g5

So White continues his plan of either getting Black to play ...h6, which
would become a weakness, or being
able to play 11 ♕d2 and then 12 h5.
Black does best to play as he did.

    10 ...   h6
    11 ♗e3   ♗d7
    12 ♕d2   ♔h7?

Black is best advised to play the
dangerous-looking 12...h5, whereupon any attempt to break on the
kingside would involve a pawn sacrifice, which is a doubtful proposi-
tion, given that Black is quite well
positioned for defence. Now, however, White has a tactical trick.

    13 h5!

Now White gets a tremendous
bind on both sides of the board.

    13 ...   g5

After 13...♘xh5? 14 g4 Black's
position collapses.

    14 a3! *(D)*

Here, it is important not to be
fooled by Black's set-up. He looks
prepared to play ...b5, but as in openings such as the Modern Benoni (see

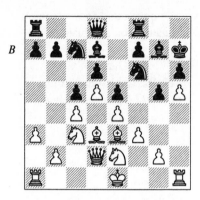

White can play on Both Sides

Chapter 6, p.119), White can get his
b4 in first. Then he will be attacking
c5, and Black will be able to do
nothing since 15...b5 loses a pawn.
So Black resorts to complete passivity, and White locks the kingside before positioning himself for the
break on the queenside.

    14 ...   b6
    15 g4!   ♘g8
    16 b4   ♔h8
    17 ♔f2   ♕f6
    18 ♔g2   ♖fb8
    19 ♖hb1   ♕d8
    20 ♖a2   ♕c8
    21 ♗c2   ♗f8
    22 ♖ab2   ♘e8 *(D)*

Although White's play to this
point has hardly been trivial, it is
easy to understand. First, he safe-
guarded his king on a side where no
action will take place for a long
time, then he doubled his rooks on
the b-file, which he intends to open,

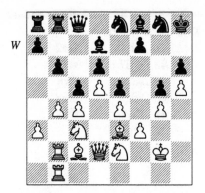

and in the meantime he has played 21 ♗c2, which is intended to fore-shadow ♗a4 to exchange his bad bishop for Black's good one; see Chapter 1. Black's last move threatens ...cxb4, which would force ♖xb4, ruining White's pawn-front, so White protects the c-pawn.

   23 **♕d3**   **♘gf6**
   24 **♘g3**   **♘g8**
   25 **♗f2**

White's plan calls for an exchange of light-squared bishops followed by bxc5 and after ...dxc5, then d6. However, as long as the black knights have access to f6, a knight can easily replace the d7-bishop as an effective blockader which at the same time inhibits action on the b-file. White's last two moves were aimed at playing ♘f5 and ♗g3 with pressure against the e-pawn. However, it is not clear just how ...f6, the move that would block in Black's knights, can be forced. That Black now voluntarily makes this damaging pawn move is a sign of lack of attention.

   25 **...**   **f6??**

After this move Black is probably lost.

   26 **♘f5**   **♘e7**
   27 **♘e3**   **♕c7**
   28 **♕d1!**

White has been jockeying to avoid exchanging either of his good knights for one of Black's bad ones. Now that the c-pawn is defended by the e3-knight, White prepares ♗a4, and the stage is set for the break.

   28 **...**   **♔h7**
   29 **♗a4**   **♘c8**
   30 **♘f5**   **♘g7** *(D)*

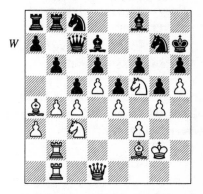

See if you can find a better location for any of White's pieces. White starts his breakthrough.

   31 **bxc5**   **♗xa4?**

After this Black is definitely lost. His only chance was 31...dxc5!, which would lead to the following beautiful variation: 32 d6! ♘xd6 33

♘d5 ♗xa4 34 ♘xc7 ♗xd1 35 ♘xd6 ♗a4! (35...♗xd6 36 ♘xa8 ♗a4 37 ♘xb6 axb6 38 ♖xb6 ♖xb6 39 ♖xb6 ♘e8 40 ♖a6 ♗b3 41 ♖a8 ♘c7 42 ♖d8 wins) 36 ♘db5! ♘e8! 37 ♘xa8 ♖xa8 38 ♘c3 ♗c6 39 ♘d5 ♘d6 40 ♖c1 ♗xd5 (40...♔g7 41 a4) 41 cxd5 ♘c8 42 a4 a5 43 ♖cb1 ♖a6 44 d6! (before Black blockades) 44...♗xd6 45 ♖d2 ♖a7 46 ♖xd6! ♘xd6 47 ♖xb6 ♘c4 48 ♖b5 ♖c7 49 ♔f1 with excellent winning chances.

32   cxb6!   ♕xc4

32...axb6 33 ♘xa4 ♘xf5 (exchanging that pesky knight and damaging White's pawn structure) would have given firmer resistance. Now Black gets routed on the queenside.

33	**♘xa4**	**axb6**
34	**♖b4**	**♕c7**
35	**♘xg7**	**♗xg7**
36	**♕b3**	**b5**
37	**♘c3!**	

There is no hurry. After 37 ♖xb5 ♖xb5 38 ♕xb5 ♕c2 Black gets a great deal of play.

37	**...**	**♘a7**
38	**♘xb5**	

This is actually a pseudo-pawn-win, as the pawn is immediately given back for a clearly won ending. The real pawn-win with 38 ♗xa7 is much less convincing as the white king is deprived of shelter from the side.

38	**...**	**♘xb5**
39	**♖xb5**	**♖xb5**
40	**♕xb5**	**♕c2**

After 40...♖xa3 41 ♕e8! and 42 ♖b8 Black get mated.

41	**♖b4!**	**♕a2**
42	**♕d7**	**♕xa3**
43	**♖b7**	**♖g8**
44	**♕e7!**	**♕a8**
45	**♖d7**	**♕f8**
46	**♕e6** *(D)*	

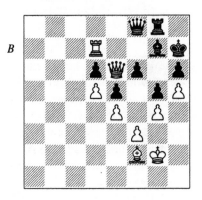

1-0

The final position deserves a diagram. Compare the quality of the two bishops.

The System when Playing Black

The System is for holding the initiative when playing White. So what does this have to do with playing Black? Actually, much of what is in this book applies to any position. It is only when we have a **System** position, that we have the mandate for finding the correct **System** move. In other positions, there are still best moves, and **System** principles can be used to find them. It is still important to deal correctly with:

a) Board control;
b) Piece placement; and
c) Evaluation of development.

If White does not play correctly, the advantage of the first move will dissipate. Black will find ways of taking advantage of this depending upon what the error is. For instance, the first move 1 e4 will sooner or later allow Black to play the counter-attack ...♘f6. Depending upon whether White chooses a passive or aggressive set-up, there will be varying ways of proceeding as Black. We examine the following strategies:

a) Counter-punching;
b) Board control by creating a colour complex while contesting the squares of the other colour.

Counter-punching

When White chooses aggression but in some incorrect manner, we see Black in counter-punching mode, meeting all of White's attempts (which are not grounded in **System** play) with solid counter-blows.

Game 5
G. Kramer – H. Berliner
New York State Ch 1949

This game was played just about the time I was discovering **The System**.

I had just become a master and was beginning to understand Options and Dynamics. In this tourney with many of the strongest US Masters in it, I tied for 2nd place with L. Evans behind M. Pavey.

1	d4	d5
2	c4	dxc4
3	♘f3	♘f6

White has given away the advantage of the first move by 3 ♘f3, which discontinues the fight for the centre, and allows Black to stop e4. Now White's edge is very minimal.

4	e3	e6
5	♗xc4	c5
6	0-0	a6
7	♕e2	b5
8	♗b3	♗b7
9	a4	♘bd7! *(D)*

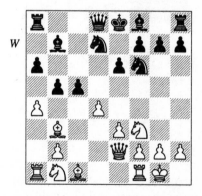

All this is standard play, although I did not know it at the time. If White now plays 10 axb5 axb5 11 ♖xa8 ♕xa8 12 ♕xb5 ♗xf3 13 gxf3 ♕xf3, Black stands well.

10 e4!

White's actual move is more speculative and Black must be careful to side-step the many tactical traps, such as 10...♗xe4 11 ♘g5 ♗d5 12 ♗xd5 ♘xd5 13 axb5 axb5 14 ♖xa8 ♕xa8 15 dxc5 with a very strong position, or 10...♘xe4 11 d5 exd5 12 ♘c3 with a vehement attack. Instead, Black quietly continues bringing his pieces out, although current analysis shows that Black stands considerably better after 10...cxd4!.

10	...	♗e7!?
11	e5	♘d5
12	axb5	axb5
13	♖xa8	♕xa8
14	dxc5	0-0! (D)

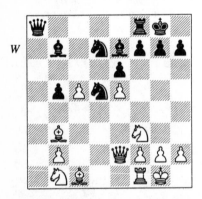

Again, there is no hurry to recapture the pawn, which would only lead to discomfort on the queenside with checks or pins. Now Black has completed his development while White's queenside is still at home.

15 ♗g5   ♗xg5!

It is interesting to study why this move is correct. The other possibility, 15...♗xc5, looks quite plausible, but leaves White with a large space advantage on the kingside and no immediate compensation. White would continue 16 ♘bd2, and then ♗c2 and ♘e4 with a dangerous attack. Instead of this, Black gets immediate strong counterplay.

| 16 | ♘xg5 | ♘f4! |
| 17 | ♕g4 (D) | |

After 17 ♕c2 g6 18 g3 h6 19 gxf4 hxg5 Black's attack is stronger than White's and good enough for at least a draw.

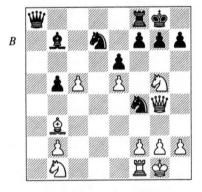

17	...	♗xg2!
18	♖e1	h6!
19	♕xf4	hxg5
20	♕xg5	♘xc5
21	♗c2	

The situation has cleared somewhat and material is even, but White still has some lingering attacking possibilities on the kingside. Black's next move sacrifices a pawn to reach a clearly drawn ending.

21	...	♗e4!
22	♗xe4	♘xe4
23	♕g4	♖c8!
24	♕xe4	♕xe4
25	♖xe4	♖c1+
26	♔g2	♖xb1
27	♖b4	g5! (D)

It is this move that makes it all work out. Now each of White's pawns is effectively isolated, and the black king can march into their midst either to win pawns or to tie up the white pieces in defending them. It is the ability to recognize such **chunking** possibilities that drives **System** thinking. It would have been safe to give up the game as drawn right now, but no one should blame my opponent for continuing.

28	♖xb5	♔g7
29	♖b3	♔g6
30	♔h3	♔h5
31	♔g2	♔g6

32	♔f3	♔f5
33	♖b7	♔g6
34	h3	♖h1
35	♔g2	♖e1
36	♖b5	♖b1
37	♖b3	♔f5
38	♖f3+	♔xe5
39	♖xf7	♖xb2
40	♔f3	♖b1

½-½

This game embodies my idea of what it means to play the black pieces. After White deviates from **System** doctrine with 3 ♘f3, leaving e4 to the black forces, Black gets free play with many counterchances. I had never seen the move 9 a4 before and was on my own after that. But it was always possible to meet every thrust of White with some counter-thrust because there were weaknesses in his position. It is true I could have punished his precocity with 10...cxd4, and in a correspondence game I am sure I would have been able to work it out. However, this does not detract much from the way the defence was set up, and that the e4-pawn, even though tactically supported, was weak and had to be advanced further. After 16...♘f4! Black's counterplay comes to a head, and the position comes down to a draw with lots of tactical flourishes and exchanges. The final point, 27...g5!, is again a show of the importance of understanding **chunking**.

The number of pawns is now relatively unimportant; it is the viable pawns that count, and White has none. His b-pawn, if it advances, only restricts the scope of its own rook, while increasing the scope of Black's. Black's pawns are viable; however, they can go nowhere, so the position can be safely judged to be a draw.

In the game below, we see what can happen if White plays a 'positional' style with no punch in it. As White gradually gives up the initiative, Black is able to react sharply and seize it himself.

Game 6
A. Bisguier – H. Berliner
US Ch, New York 1957/8

> 1   d4   ♘f6
> 2   ♘f3

As all readers will immediately recognize, White's 2 ♘f3 is already a non-**System** move, and should allow Black to equalize. Black chooses the king's fianchetto defence as he now no longer needs to fear the Sämisch Variation (5 f3).

> 2   ...   g6
> 3   ♗f4

White continues to go his original merry way, possibly hoping to throw his opponent on his own resources. However, this move is a serious positional error. Black will play ...d6

eventually, and thereafter the f4-bishop will be subject to attacks involving Black playing ...e5.

> 3   ...   ♗g7
> 4   ♘bd2   0-0
> 5   e4   d6
> 6   c3   ♘c6
> 7   ♗c4 *(D)*

After Black's 6...♘c6! White cannot play 7 d5 as 7...e5! frees Black's game completely. So White continues his development with 7 ♗c4.

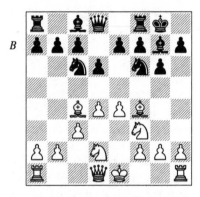

It is time to take stock. Black has essentially completed his development except for the queen and rooks, as the c8-bishop is really quite active and there is no better place for it at the moment. White, on the other hand, still has not castled, and there are possibilities for exploiting this if the e-file can be opened. By our method of counting development, White's count is –4 (rooks, queen, and castling), while Black's count is –3 (rooks and queen). Further, it is

Black's move. With a 1.5 lead in development, is it any wonder that he can do some tactical things here in his bid for scope in the centre?

So Black's 7...e5! comes only as a mild surprise. It does require some accurate tactical calculation, but the fact that this move may be good should come as no surprise. After the move, Black is at least equal. White would be better advised to play 9 ♗e3, and keep the e-file closed, but he did not see the full import of Black's play, and thought that 7...e5 was a pawn sacrifice.

7	...	e5!
8	dxe5	dxe5
9	♘xe5?	♘xe5
10	♗xe5	♘xe4!

At first this move looks unplayable, but I was able to find it when deciding on 7...e5, based upon my belief that the dynamics of the position had shifted to Black with his 1.5 move lead in development.

11 ♗xg7 ♖e8! (D)

With this move (instead of the losing 11...♔xg7?) Black unveils his secret weapon on the e-file, and threatens to win the queen with ...♘xc3+.

12	♗e2	♔xg7
13	♘xe4	♕xd1+
14	♖xd1	♖xe4
15	♖d8??	

White's plans have come to nothing, after which the game is essentially even. However, in the mistaken

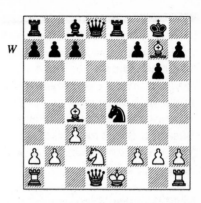

belief that White still had something to play for, Bisguier now plays a horrible blunder that loses a pawn and the game. However, more to the point, even after the more sensible 15 f3 ♖e8 16 ♔f2 ♗e6 Black has the better of a clear draw.

15	...	♖xe2+
16	♔xe2	♗g4+
17	f3	♗xf3+

...and Black won.

This is a wonderful illustration of how the dynamics of positions work. White plays passively, and Black breaks out with at least equality.

Game 7
A. Ericson – H. Berliner
*5th World Correspondence Ch
Final, 1965-8*

1 e4 ♘f6

If White's only correct **System** first move is 1 d4, then how should one proceed against the inferior 1 e4? I believe this is a matter of taste. It is clear that the e4-pawn is not well defended, and subject to counter-attack. Whether one first fixes the pawn by 1...e5, restrains it by 1...d6, or attacks it right away seems to be a matter of style, although it must be said that the Alekhine Defence seems to have hit upon hard times these days. However, in 1965 not that much was understood about how White should proceed.

2	e5	♘d5
3	d4	d6
4	♘f3	g6
5	♗e2	♗g7
6	c4	♘b6
7	exd6	cxd6

White has not chosen a very enterprising plan. He avoided 4 c4 ♘b6 5 f4, which I believe is best. Also, Black's enterprising 4...g6 is best met by 5 ♗c4. Now Black gives White the pawn majority in the centre. He does have something in mind in doing this. However, one must realize that his play is hardly **Systemic** in that he is developing randomly, hoping for stray tactical chances based upon the games and analysis of his predecessors.

8	h3	0-0
9	0-0	♘c6
10	♘c3	♗f5!

Black refuses to commit himself with either ...e5 or ...d5, until White plays ♗e3 or b3.

| 11 | ♗e3 | d5! |

Here comes the counter-attack! The point is that when the knight arrives at c4 it will be threatening the e3-bishop and thus force White to do something about this. If White now plays 12 cxd5 ♘xd5 Black has a very comfortable game with his fianchettoed bishop observing the isolated d-pawn as in a Tarrasch Defence with colours reversed.

| 12 | c5 | ♘c4 |
| 13 | ♗xc4 | |

Another possibility is 13 ♗c1 b6! 14 b3 bxc5 15 bxc4 cxd4 16 cxd5 (16 ♘xd5 loses to 16...d3) 16...dxc3 17 dxc6 ♕xd1 18 ♖xd1 ♗g4 with a big advantage for Black.

13	...	dxc4
14	d5	♘b4
15	♗d4!	(D)

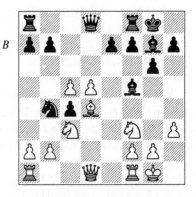

B

An excellent idea in a near-desperate position. White attempts to capitalize on his only asset: his central pawn structure. At the time of this game, I felt very secure in the idea that Black was vastly superior. Much later I found out that some analyses, including one by Keres, purported to show that White is better. I find that truly amazing. Black is clearly better according to all **System** principles. He has the two bishops, excellent play for his minor pieces against a doubtful white centre, and there are prospects of winning a centre pawn. All he need do is to avoid some premature win of material instead of pursuing the attack on the centre. Of course, the published analysis seemed to think Black should play to win material. Now, we show how Black gets a winning advantage.

15 ...   &d3!

But not 15...&xd4 16 ♕xd4! ♘c2 17 ♕xc4 ♘xa1 18 ♖xa1 and White is better.

16 &xg7   ♔xg7
17 ♖e1   ♕c7!

Black does well to resist 17...♘c2? 18 ♘e5 ♘xe1 19 ♕xe1 ♕c7 20 ♕e3, when White's potent centre will make it difficult for Black to use his rooks effectively. The destruction of the centre must have first priority. It is the ability to discern such things that makes for great play. Nothing in this book (except possibly this example) can prepare you to make such decisions. It should be apparent though, that in the line above, White has a very good centre, and Black's rooks will be subjugated for some

time. That should be enough to be wary of winning an exchange, when the win of a pawn is at hand.

18 ♖e5   f6!

Necessary. After 18...♕xc5 19 a3 ♘a6 Black gets good play against the e-pawn. White's next move is virtually forced.

19 d6   exd6
20 cxd6

20 ♘d4 does not work because of 20...♕d7 21 ♘e6+ ♔g8, when White is over-extended.

20 ...   ♕xd6
21 ♖b5   b6
22 a3 (D)

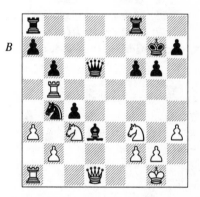

Where does the knight go?

Black must decide where to retreat his knight.

22 ...   ♘a6!

This strange-looking move is the best of the game. Its full ramifications will not be apparent for another ten moves. Suffice it to say that study convinced me that the knight needed a secure anchoring point, which it can achieve at c5 but not from c6. For instance, after 22...♘c6 23 ♖d5 ♕e6 24 ♕a4 to be followed by 25 ♖e1, Black's position is very loose. However, the move does involve a planned return of the pawn, in order to get a position where White's pieces will be tied up, while Black's roam freely.

23   ♖d5   ♕e7
24   ♘e1   ♗f5!

The first point of 22...♘a6; White can have the c-pawn if he wants it. 24...♘c5 25 b4 is no good for Black.

25   ♕a4   ♘c5
26   ♕xc4   ♗e6
27   ♕e2   ♖fe8
28   ♖dd1   ♘b3! (D)

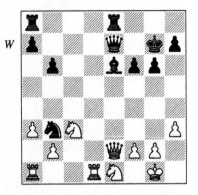

Since 25 ♕a4, all moves have been forced for both sides. Possibly White has been congratulating himself on re-establishing material equality; however, such joy should be

short-lived. The point of giving up the c-pawn now becomes apparent; the a1-rook will be trapped and the exchange will eventually be lost.

29   ♖ab1   ♗f5
30   ♕b5

I had spent most of my time working out the ramifications of 30 ♕xe7+ ♖xe7 31 ♘d3, when 31...♖d8! 32 ♘b4 ♖de8 33 ♘d3 (33 ♘cd5 ♖f7 34 ♘d3 ♖d7 35 ♘5f4 ♖ed8) 33...♘c5 34 ♘d5 ♗xd3 wins. The important thing is to avoid 31...♘c5 32 ♘d5, when the rook has no safe square, e.g., 32...♖f7 33 ♘xc5 ♗xb1 34 ♘e6+. But the text-move is no salvation either.

30   ...   ♕f7!
31   ♘d3   ♖ad8

Black threatens to win material with 32...♗xd3 33 ♖xd3 a6! 34 ♕xa6 ♘c5. So White must finally part with the exchange.

32   ♘f4   ♗xb1
33   ♖xb1   ♖e5
34   ♕c6   ♕d7
35   ♕xd7+   ♖xd7

White played on for another 17 moves, but he could have resigned here. A game full of interesting strategic decisions that involve chunks and their interaction.

The Board-Control Strategy

Another defensive strategy for Black that has become very popular due to the post-war influence of the Soviet players is playing the King's Indian Defence in order to control the dark squares as the game goes on. This hypermodern strategy is always useful, and is certainly advocated when playing Black and under no obligation to control the whole board. The following games give examples of how one side takes control of the squares of one colour and uses his ability to own one-half of the board to gradually take over the whole board.

Game 8
V. Zita – D. Bronstein
Prague – Moscow match 1946

This is one of the original 'board-control smashes' that put the new way of playing the King's Indian Defence on the map. Black's play is magnificent, although by today's standards, White plays rather ineptly in his attempt to deal with what was then a brand new opening.

| 1 | c4 | e5 |

White starts out in a **non-Systemic** way, and Black prevents his getting back in.

| 2 | ♘c3 | ♘f6 |
| 3 | ♘f3 | |

Now it is too late to worry about controlling e4. The position is heading for a non-board-controlling situation.

| 3 | ... | d6 |

| 4 | d4 | ♘bd7 |
| 5 | g3 | |

This is the same mistake as in Game 9, Evans-Berliner. The bishop does not belong on the long diagonal if White is going to have to block it by e4. The more modest development by ♗e2 is much better.

5	...	g6
6	♗g2	♗g7
7	0-0	0-0 *(D)*

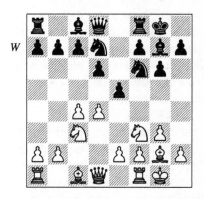

| 8 | b3 | |

This move is not to be recommended. White must prepare to defend d4, against which Black will mass his counterplay. The bishop on b2 may appear to help in this, but only if the c3-knight moves. 8 h3 followed by ♗e3, as in the following game, is much better.

| 8 | ... | c6 |

This move is not the most accurate, as now White could cause some discomfort with 9 ♗a3. Better was 8...♖e8.

9 &b2   &e8
10 e4   exd4
11 ⦿xd4   ♛b6!

The beginning of a strategy to take over the dark squares. This move exerts pressure on d4 and stops White playing b4, which could chase away the knight that is about to take up residence at c5.

12 ♛d2   ⦿c5
13 &fe1   a5!
14 &ab1   a4!

Having secured the dark squares, Black begins to expand on the queenside, taking advantage of the fact that White cannot play b4 to fix the white pawns on b3 and c4, where they will remain targets.

15 &a1   axb3
16 axb3   ⦿g4!

Black begins what is already the final attack. Note how the correct method of assessing development finds that the 'undeveloped' a8-rook and c8-bishop are both beautifully poised to contribute, whereas the 'developed' b1-rook and e1-rook are only defending and not really developed in pursuit of any meaningful objective. This is dynamics at its very best.

17 h3?

It is instructive to do a development count: White's is −2 (the two rooks), while Black's is 0. So Black is 2.5 moves ahead. Now Black shatters the illusion that the white position is held together, and that his

centre is secure. The motive for the denouement is really quite easy to understand. The only really useful piece that White has is the a1-bishop, which is trying to defend the dark squares. It is defended by the b1-rook, which is overloaded since it must also help defend b3, where a knight fork could take place.

17 ...   &xa1!!
18 &xa1   ⦿xf2!! (D)

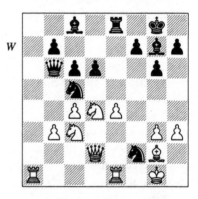

The move lays bare the g1-a7 diagonal, which will result in the d4-knight becoming pinned if the f2-knight is captured. On 19 ♛xf2, 19...⦿d3 is winning; and on 19 &xf2, 19...⦿xb3 is deadly. So White continues hopelessly behind in material.

19 &e3   ⦿xh3+
20 &h2   ⦿f2
21 &f3   ⦿cxe4
22 ♛f4   ⦿g4+
23 &h1   f5!

The positional end of the game. Black has bishop and three pawns for a rook, which is an overwhelming material advantage, and White has no play at all.

24	♘xe4	♖xe4
25	♕xd6	♖xd4
26	♕b8	♖d8
27	♖a8	♗e5
28	♕a7	♕b4
29	♕g1	♕f8
30	♗h3	♕h6

0-1

In the following game, White improves upon Zita's play. However, Black allows White's pressure, but makes sure to hold on to the dark squares, which will guarantee him a major say about how the game will turn out. With the white king's bishop fianchettoed, Black almost always has this option (see also the previous game).

Game 9
L. Evans – H. Berliner
Western Open Ch, Milwaukee 1957

1	d4	♘f6
2	c4	g6
3	g3	

With this move White departs the **System** path and now must reconcile himself to finding advantages where he can. This line of play has now almost completely disappeared from master play.

3	...	♗g7
4	♗g2	0-0

5	e4	d6
6	♘e2	e5
7	0-0	c6
8	♘bc3	♘bd7
9	h3 *(D)*	

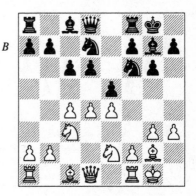

The play up to Black's 13th move is fairly standard. At this point Black gives up the centre to get play against the pawns and pieces there.

9	...	exd4
10	♘xd4	♖e8
11	♗e3	♘c5
12	♕c2	a5
13	♖ad1	♘fd7
14	♘b3!	♕c7!

With 13...♘fd7 Black wants to play ...♘e5 and force some weakness on the white queenside in defending the c4-pawn. However, White meets this in excellent fashion. Black would be ill-advised to play 14...♘xb3 15 axb3, after which he would have no play on the queenside. Instead, he invites White to double Black's c-pawns, which is

also not a good idea for White as then Black would wield full control over the dark squares.

15	♖d2	a4!
16	♘xc5	♘xc5
17	♖fd1 *(D)*	

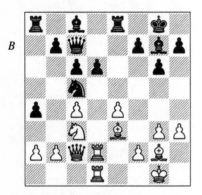

B

Black must decide how to proceed. To defend with 17...♗f8 18 ♗f4 would be senseless; so Black, having said A must now say B, and kiss his d-pawn goodbye. However, the next move puts a great deal of pressure on White's queenside. White is forced to part with his best piece, the dark-squared bishop, after which Black wields control over the dark squares.

17	...	♕a5!
18	♖xd6	a3!
19	♗xc5	♕xc5
20	b3	♗e6!

Without his dark-squared bishop, White is subject to all sorts of buffeting on both the light and dark squares. Despite his extra pawn, he must

struggle to keep his head above water against the coming queenside attack with ...b5!. He tries a tactical skirmish, hoping Black will back away.

21	♘a4	♖xa4!
22	bxa4	♕xc4
23	♕xc4	♗xc4
24	♖6d2	♗b2!
25	♖b1	♖a8

½-½

Black has easy play for a draw.

Taking Control of Wing Squares

This is a very attractive game. My opponent here was Bob Steinmeyer, long one of the leading OTB players in the US, and second ranked to me in the US in correspondence play. The occasion was a four-game play-off match for the 1959 Golden Knights Championship, which was the strongest correspondence tourney held in the US each year. I won the play-off by the score of 3½-½.

Game 10
R. H. Steinmeyer – H. Berliner
Golden Knights Ch Play-off 1959

1	d4	♘f6
2	c4	g6
3	♘c3	♗g7
4	e4	d6
5	f3	c6
6	♗e3	a6

7	♕d2	b5
8	♗d3	

The Byrne variation (7...b5) is my favourite way of meeting the Sämisch Variation (5 f3) of the King's Indian Defence. White takes a passive, but not necessarily bad approach.

8	...	♘bd7
9	♘ge2	0-0
10	0-0	e5
11	a3	exd4?

Premature; 11...♗b7 is correct.

12	♘xd4	♗b7
13	a4! *(D)*	

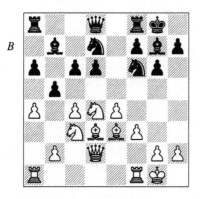

13	...	b4

With this move Black embarks (is forced into) a dark-square strategy. The c5-square can now no longer be controlled by white pawns, so Black prepares to use it by pieces, and White should play so as to prevent this.

14	♘ce2	a5!
15	♖ac1?	

This is a distinct error due to a view of perfunctorily deploying the pieces without examining an overall strategy. White should play 15 ♘b3 and organize pressure on the d-file.

15	...	♘c5
16	b3?	

This is a strategic error which counterbalances Black's error on move 11. The b3-square is needed for the white knight so it can challenge the c5-knight.

16	...	♖e8
17	♘f4	♖c8!!

A 'mysterious rook move' in the style of Nimzowitsch. The c5-knight will be in need of protection after an eventual ...d5, cxd5.

18	♖fd1	

White is playing without a plan, and Black equalizes easily by threatening and eventually enforcing the ...d5 advance.

18	...	♕e7
19	♖e1	♕f8!
20	♗f1	d5! *(D)*

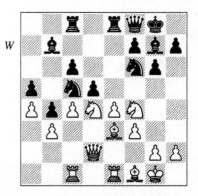

Black takes the Initiative

Black's 20...d5 was fully prepared. Now Black is at least equal; White's b3-pawn is a great liability.

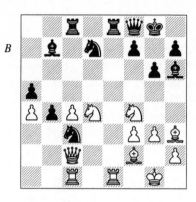

21 exd5   cxd5
22 ♕f2?   ♘ce4!

Taking advantage of White's mistake on move 22. If he now plays 23 fxe4, then comes 23...♘g4 24 ♕d2 ♖xe4 and one of White's three minor pieces in the centre will be lost.

23 ♕c2   ♘c3

At this point I was recalling the famous game Réti-Capablanca, New York 1924. Réti intruded with his knight in a similar way and beat Capablanca. With the dark squares on the queenside firmly under his control, Black now embarks upon controlling the rest of the board.

24 ♗f2   ♗h6!
25 g3   dxc4!
26 bxc4

After 26 ♗xc4, Black can play 26...♘fd5! 27 ♘xd5 ♗xd5. Now the knight is denied d5, but the queenside comes alive, with a knight on c5 again playing a pivotal role.

26 ...   ♘d7!
27 ♗h3 (D)
27 ...   f5

It looks as if this is very weakening, but in reality a white knight on e6 is biting nothing.

28 ♘b5!?

White struggles to remove the bone (the c3-knight) in his throat, but now there will be opposing queenside connected passed pawns, and

Black's will be mobile and White's not.

28 ...   ♘xb5
29 axb5   ♘c5
30 ♖xe8   ♖xe8
31 ♗g2

White's pieces are in a sorry state, while Black's are blooming.

31 ...   a4!
32 ♖d1   a3!!

This is possible because of many tactical nuances.

33 ♕d2   b3!
34 ♕b4 (D)

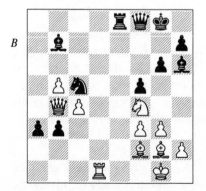

This apparently saving multiple attack does not work because of the coming queen sacrifice.

34 ...	a2!!
35 ♗xc5	♕xc5+!
36 ♕xc5	b2

At this moment Black is a queen down, and it is his opponent's turn to play. Yet White is quite lost. A unique position in practical chess play.

| 37 ♕f2 | b1♕ |
| 38 ♕f1 | ♕xd1! |

Another queen sacrifice, but this one was easy.

| 39 ♕xd1 | ♖a8 |
| 40 c5 | |

After 40 ♕a1 comes 40...♗g7.

40 ...	a1♕
41 ♕xa1	♖xa1+
42 ♔f2	♗xf4
	0-1

After 43 gxf4 ♗d5 White's pawns are going nowhere.

The Struggle for Colour Dominance

In previous sections, we showed examples of board control arising out of the King's Indian Defence where Black challenges d4 with ...e5 and waits for the correct moment of take on d4, thereby creating the potential of controlling the dark squares. In this and the next section, the struggle for colour dominance takes less usual forms that are quite instructive.

Game 11

H. de Carbonnel – H. Berliner
5th World Correspondence Ch Final, 1965-8

1 d4	♘f6
2 c4	g6
3 ♘c3	♗g7
4 e4	d6
5 f3	c6
6 ♗e3	a6
7 ♕d2	b5

This is the Byrne variation which I regularly use to combat the Sämisch variation of the King's Indian Defence. It leaves much room for contesting the squares on the queenside and in the centre. Black chooses an aggressive reply recommended in the books because it has led to some quick OTB wins for White. Whether 8 0-0-0 is best seems doubtful (see Chapter 5, p.104).

8 0-0-0	♕a5
9 ♔b1	♘bd7
10 g4	♖b8
11 h4	

White's last two moves constituted the latest attempt at the time to push through the white attack on the king. However, Black can maintain his king safety easily as shown and need only sit in a somewhat cramped position for a few moves while he completes his development.

11 ...	h5!
12 g5	♘h7
13 ♖h2	

Here and in the next few moves White plays too passively. Correct was 13 f4.

13 ...   ♘hf8

Black uses the opportunity to re-activate his knight, but this move is not quite correct as White could now introduce favourable complications with 14 e5!. Instead, his next move cedes the advantage to Black.

14 ♖c1   ♘b6
15 cxb5?

15 c5 must be played, when after 15...dxc5 16 dxc5 ♘c4 17 ♗xc4 bxc4 18 ♗d4 ♘e6 19 ♗xg7 ♘xg7 20 ♕d4 0-0 21 ♕xc4 ♖b4 Black re-tains the advantage despite the pawn minus. The text creates an open a-file for Black, which will become very important.

15 ...   axb5
16 ♘d1   ♕a8!
17 f4   ♘c4!
18 ♗xc4   bxc4 *(D)*

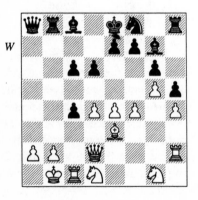

19 ♖f2

Naturally the pawn cannot be taken because of 19...♗e6. Now Black has two open files against the white king. But here White had to play 19 ♘c3 to protect his centre against the coming attack.

Let us sum up the positional val-ues in the style of Chapter 3.

a) White's development count is −2 (the two knights), although it is euphoric to consider the white king as being in a secure position with two open files with black major pieces on them bearing down on him.

b) Black's count is −3 (king, knight, h8-rook), so with Black to move, he is 0.5 tempi behind.

c) White is not threatening to capture on c4, as the reply ...♗e6 is much too strong. However, if White could play f5, he would be able to contest a significant part of the board.

d) The value of the central board control chunk is about +0.5.

e) The value of the white king-safety chunk is about −1.0 with the current amount of material on the board.

f) The value of the black king-safety chunk is 0.0.

However, all the above really avoids the main issue, which is who is controlling the space on the board. White appears to be controlling the centre, but his e4-pawn is unsup-ported, and subject to attack. Fur-ther, if Black can open up the a1-h8 long diagonal for his bishop, then it too will be participating in the pressure on the white monarch. So, the essence of the position is what will happen in the centre, and now is the time for Black to pose the question.

19 ...   c5!!

This is the fly in the ointment. How is the e4-pawn (and all it means in terms of controlling the board) to be supported? If 20 d5 then the critical a1-h8 diagonal has been opened and Black simply plays 20...♘d7 and continues his queenside attack as in the Benko Gambit with the additional bonus that the white king is also a target. The fact that the c4-pawn is lost will play absolutely no role in all this as Black brings all of his pieces to bear on the queenside, while White can only await developments.

Therefore, it seems best for White to try to steady his centre with 20 ♘c3 and seek to turn his current advantage in space to some account.

20 ♘c3   ♘e6! *(D)*

Black is unrelenting. White will have to make a major concession in the centre. Now 21 ♘ge2 cxd4 22 ♗xd4 (22 ♘xd4 loses to 22...♘c5!) 22...♘xd4 23 ♘xd4 0-0 gives Black a wonderful position. Also, 21 d5 ♘d4 is hardly to be considered. So White decides to give up the centre, and hopes to damage Black's pawn structure or else win some pawns.

21 dxc5   ♗b7!

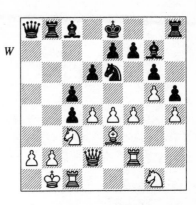

Now the white centre is blasted apart. The light squares are going to change hands, and this will in a few moves leave a situation where Black controls the light squares, while the dark squares are on dispute on the kingside. However, on the queenside, where it really matters, Black is in charge of both coloured squares.

22 cxd6

White dare not countenance 22 ♕c2, as after 22...dxc5 the threat of ...♘d4 is much too strong.

22 ...   ♗xe4+
23 ♔a1   0-0!
24 dxe7   ♖fe8 *(D)*

Material is not important. All of Black's pieces will now assume meaningful roles, while those of White sit passively by. White is temporarily two pawns ahead in material, but even if he can keep only one, it is important to understand what Black has achieved in return for his material deficit. A chunk analysis is in order:

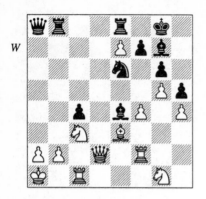

a) Chunk (White's king safety): −1.5. The white king is very insecure and White cannot play ♘xe4 as this opens the long diagonal for the other bishop.

b) Chunk (Black's king safety): 0.0. It is interesting to note how steady Black's king safety is. The white pawns are knocking at the portal, so to speak, but there is no way of enforcing f5, and thus they remain as mere bystanders.

c) Chunk (White's e3-bishop): −0.5. This bishop has only defensive roles to play.

d) Chunk (White's g1-knight): −0.25. It is not clear how this knight will participate.

It is clear that Black has more than enough compensation for his present two-pawn deficit. However, the e7-pawn will certainly be lost, which will leave him with even less compensation for his positional problems. His only hope is to be able to effect some exchanges while Black

is capturing the e7-pawn, so as to lessen the effect of the attack on the king.

25 ♕d1

The main line was 25 ♕d7 ♗f5 26 ♕a7 (not 26 ♕a4 ♕xa4 27 ♘xa4 ♖xe7 28 ♖xc4 ♘d4!) 26...♕xa7 27 ♗xa7 ♖a8 28 ♗e3 ♖xe7 (threatening ...♘xg5) 29 ♖e2 ♗d3 30 ♖ee1 ♗d4! (threatening ...♘c5) 31 a3 ♗xc3! 32 ♖xc3 ♘d4 and wins. After the text-move, Black wins by force.

25 ...	♖xe7
26 ♘f3	♖d8
27 ♘d2 (D)	

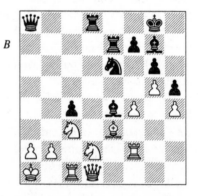

27 ...   ♘d4!

It still seems incredible that the natural 27...♗d3, which consolidates all advantages and maintains the excellent bishop, does not seem to lead anywhere. But after 28 ♕a4 Black will have to exchange queens. Although he can recover his sacrificed pawn, White will escape with only a small positional disadvantage. The text-move appears to be the only way of increasing Black's advantage. Black gives up some positional pressure for a forced gain of material.

28 ♗xd4

This move is forced as otherwise the attack on the white king becomes far too strong; i.e. 28 ♘cxe4 ♘b3+ 29 ♔b1 ♘xc1 30 ♕xc1 ♖xe4 31 ♘xe4 (31 ♘xc4 ♗d4!) 31...♕xe4+ 32 ♖c2 (32 ♔a1 ♕xe3) 32...c3 33 b3 ♕f3 wins.

28	...	♗xd4
29	♘dxe4	♗xf2
30	♕c2	

After 30 ♕f3 ♗d4 the threat of ...♗xc3 forces White to realign his troops again.

30	...	♗e3
31	♖f1	♖d3!
32	♘f6+	♔g7
33	f5	♖e5 *(D)*

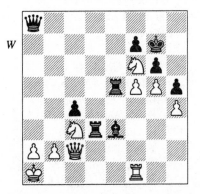

To avoid the threat of ♘xh5+ followed by f6+. Now, White will see if he can successfully attack the black king. After much investigation on move 27, it was my judgement that he could not. However, the game is in a delicate state because Black traded his positional advantages for material, and must now see if he can defend all threats.

34	fxg6	fxg6
35	♕h2	♕b8!
36	♖b1!	

I was hoping White would meet the threat of ...♖d2 with 36 ♘fe4 ♖f5 37 ♕xb8 ♖xf1+ 38 ♘b1 ♖xb1+ 39 ♔xb1 ♖d1+ 40 ♔c2 ♖c1#. However, the excellent defensive move in text forces Black to become inventive again in order to garner the full point.

36	...	♖b5!
37	♕h1	♗d4!!

This is the key idea. The d4-bishop is a giant of a bishop. It controls the whole board and is the key to the attack on the white monarch, which now resumes even while Black's king is also under attack. However, the bishop controls both sides of the board. White must take the rook, as otherwise he has no compensation while his position keeps getting worse.

38	♘xb5	♕xb5
39	♕h2	♕b7!

Meets the immediate infiltration threats of the queen, and renews the deadly threat of ...c3. White must do something immediately.

40	♘e8+	♚h8
41	♘d6	♕d5!
42	♕f4	♖f3!
43	♕e4 *(D)*	

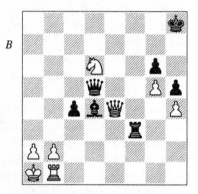

White's last hope to simplify the position and avoid the mating attack. However:

43	...	c3!!
44	♕e8+	

Clearly, White cannot play 44 ♕xd5 cxb2+ 45 ♖xb2 ♖f1#. However, the time for remedies is long past.

44	...	♚h7
45	♕e7+	♗g7
46	bxc3	♕xd6!

It was important for Black not to be lured by 46...♖xc3?? 47 ♘e8! ♖c7+ 48 ♘f6+ and White mates.

0-1

After 47 ♕xd6, 47...♖xc3+ mates.

A game that shows dynamics extremely well. I had to reject the intuitively appealing 27...♗d3, because in the absence of concrete variations

one must take the material gain that is available. The middlegame, in which Black controls the whole board while being a pawn behind, is worthy of study.

Keeping Control of the Critical Central Squares

In the following example, Black plays some very strange moves. If it were not for a very crisp set of replies, Black could well have got a fine game by taking over all the important dark squares. Thus, this is an example of how to thwart the attempt to create a colour complex. The key to an understanding of this game is the notion of controlling certain squares, which if the opponent were to take them over would spell catastrophe. In this game the key square is e5. After maintaining control of e5, the simple principles of development and piece placement made the rest easy.

Game 12
H. Berliner – S. Fazekas
*5th World Correspondence Ch,
Semi-Final 1, 1962-5*

1	d4	♘f6
2	c4	e6
3	♘c3	♗b4
4	♗g5	

I have indicated at several points in this book that I do not know what the correct 4th move for White is in this position. I know that 4 &g5 is not correct as it violates several of the principles. But rather than a play a 'principled' move that I do not know how to follow up, I have been playing 4 &g5 for many years now.

> **4 ...   h6**
> **5 &h4   &xc3+**

I find it amazing that anyone should voluntarily give up such a bishop for a knight just to double the c-pawns. If this is to be done, it should be after White has expended a tempo to force it. White certainly has better things to do than to play &c1 or &c2 which would prevent the doubling, but lose time, so the black 'threat' to double the pawns will not go away.

> **6 bxc3   &e7**

Again, a strange and passive-looking move. It is difficult to discern whether or not Black has any plan. White now intends to take over the whole centre, but a fight is brewing.

> **7 f3!   d5** *(D)*

Again a strange-looking move. It would appear as if Black wants to play a dark-square strategy which entails playing ...d6 and ...e5. However, this would leave most of the centre to White. But it will soon become apparent that Black has a more grandiose plan.

> **8 &c2   &bd7**
> **9 e4   dxe4**
> **10 fxe4   e5**

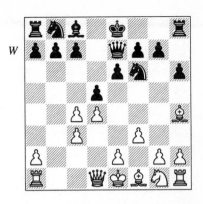

This was Black's intention. The pressure on the e4-pawn can become very strong, and White is forced to sacrifice a pawn if he does not want to succumb to a colour complex.

> **11 &d3!   exd4**
> **12 cxd4   c5**
> **13 &f3!**

If White here played routinely to conserve material with d5, then he would cede to Black control of all the dark central squares, and with it any hope of obtaining an advantage. In fact, after 13 d5?, Black would have the dynamic advantage of being able to control the dark central squares while White would be occupying the light central squares with pawns, which would bring in nothing.

> **13 ...   cxd4**
> **14 0-0!!** *(D)*

Not, of course, 14 &xd4, after which the white centre is as full of holes as a Swiss cheese, and his position very precarious.

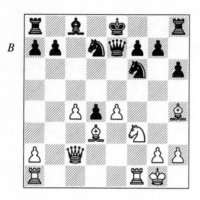

B

The black d4-pawn actually helps stabilize the white centre as Black's pieces cannot now use the square. This is an important strategic idea.

If we now take stock, we can see that White's development is −1 (only the a1-rook needs developing), while Black's is −5 (castling, king's rook, queen's rook, queen's bishop [2]). So White is 3.5 tempi ahead for a pawn, and also has the bishop-pair, plus Black's king is rather insecure. A computer may take note of White's three isolated pawns; however, this is not of much account. What is important is not that they are isolated, but that the squares in front of them are of no use to Black; which in effect means they are not weak.

However, Black is in desperate need to find places for his pieces, and his king position is cause for concern. Any freeing attempt by Black such as 14...g5 15 ♗f2! would make his king position even less secure, and allow White to smoothly take control of the central dark squares too. Moves such as 14...♘e5 also do not work as then would come 15 ♘xe5 ♕xe5 16 ♗g3 followed by e5 with a tremendous game for White. On 14...0-0, 15 e5! ♘xe5 16 ♖ae1 ♘xf3+ 17 ♖xf3 ♗e6 18 ♗xf6 gxf6 19 ♕d2 ♔g7 20 ♖g3+ wins immediately. Black must face up to the threat of 15 e5 which would win a knight, so he must do something to relieve the pin.

14	...	♕c5
15	♖ab1!	♘g4
16	♖b5	♕a3
17	♕b3! *(D)*	

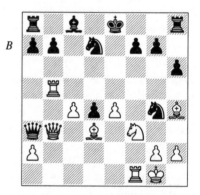

B

Very unexpected, I am sure. White sees his future in an endgame with a very superior development and his two bishops.

17	...	♕xb3
18	axb3	a6
19	♖a1!	

White's pieces are all beautifully placed, while Black's are either at home or flailing thin air. The fact that Black could never find adequate locations for his pieces was at the heart of the remainder of the game, which Black lost without ever really being in the competition.

Knowing When to take Chances

When playing White it is clear that I advocate playing **The System**, which, when fully developed, should be a path for maintaining the advantage of the first move indefinitely. However, what is one to do when playing Black? It makes a difference as to whether one is playing in a tournament or match. In a match it is quite satisfactory to draw with Black and expect to gain your points when playing White. However, in a tournament, especially one in which one is hoping for first place, it may be necessary to take some chances. It is possible to play Black in a conservative manner, hoping that the opponent misses the best continuation, and thus expecting to equalize the position. From there on, one can hope to outplay the opponent and eventually score the point.

However, it is also possible to take risks. Risks come in many shapes and sizes. In correspondence play, I have found that during my career in the 1960s, the top correspondence players were, with certain notable exceptions, not among the class of OTB IMs or GMs. These players were able to calculate well when required, but lacked a little in positional understanding, and in their overall understanding of opening play. For the latter, they relied mainly on opening books, which, if you are a top OTB player, you will know are just a compendium, but hardly a bible of what is best. So in correspondence play it is possible to play obscure lines about which one knows something that has not yet been documented in opening books.

Clearly, there is real risk in this. Usually, an opening has a 'bad' reputation for good reason. Also, the opponent may have found out about a 'bust' that is not in the book, or even found his own 'bust'. However, knowing when to risk is an art, and it must be cultivated by experience. In the game below, I ventured the Alekhine Defence, and especially an unusual 4th move. This move had purportedly been refuted, and the 'refutation', 5 ♘g5, was in all the opening books. When this move was first sprung on me by Curt Braskett at the Champion of Champions tourney in 1957, I did not play the correct 6...♗g7, but was able to escape with a draw. Thereafter, I continued to examine this 5 ♘g5?! 'refutation', until I found it was not a refutation at all, but led to inferiority for White.

I now began employing 4...g6 again, and garnered a few points with my new move. Also, I won several correspondence games with it. However, about 1965 a new 'refutation' was found, and this was 5 ♗c4!. After this move, neither 5...♘b6 6 ♗b3 ♗g7 7 ♘g5! d5 8 f4 nor 5...c6 6 0-0 ♗g7 7 ♕e2 with a big space advantage is completely satisfactory for Black. I had already lost one game and drawn one against 5 ♗c4 in OTB play, but it was a new move, and I was sure that few players would know about this (of course, nowadays with current databases this is no longer possible).

So I employed the Alekhine Defence four times in the Final of the 5th Correspondence World Championship, and won all four games. In three of them, the move 4...g6 was played. The game below was one of these, and it is instructive what happens to White as he gradually realizes that he has been led down the garden path to an unhappy end.

Game 13
Altschuler – H. Berliner
*5th World Correspondence Ch
Final, 1965-8*

1	e4	♘f6
2	e5	♘d5
3	d4	d6
4	♘f3	g6?!
5	♘g5?	dxe5!

| 6 | dxe5 | ♗g7! *(D)* |

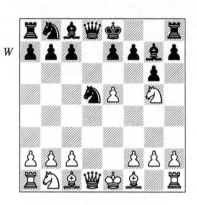

7 ♗c4
White now realizes that the intended 7 c4 does not work. In a game Dannberg-Berliner, 5th World Correspondence Ch Semi-Final, 1962-5, the continuation was 7...♘b4! 8 ♕xd8+ ♔xd8. After 9 ♘xf7+ ♔e8 10 ♘xh8 ♘c2+ 11 ♔d1 ♘xa1 12 ♗d3 (12 ♘xg6 ♗f5!) 12...♗f5 13 ♗xf5 gxf5 14 f4 ♘c6 the a1-knight would survive, i.e. 15 ♗e3 ♘b4 16 ♘a3 ♘xa2. White therefore played 9 ♘a3, when 9...♔e8 gave Black an excellent game.

| 7 | ... | c6 |
| 8 | ♕e2 | |

The attempt to make something out of the situation occurred in Stern-Berliner (in the same tournament), which continued 8 ♘c3 h6! 9 ♘xf7 ♔xf7 10 ♘xd5 cxd5 11 ♗xd5+ ♔e8! 12 e6 ♖f8 and Black had a winning position. Here again one sees the difference between correspondence play and OTB. If this had occurred in an OTB tourney, all players would have access to games played in earlier rounds. In correspondence play, unless there is much discussion among players, each game is a new experience.

| 8 | ... | h6 |
| 9 | ♘f3 | ♗g4 *(D)* |

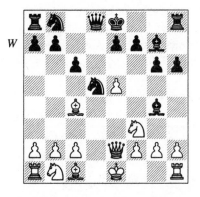

Black now has a position that could have been reached from a Pirc Defence where White is a move behind and Black has ...h6 thrown in for good measure. Compare this position with the one in the introductory comments when White plays the correct 5 ♗c4. Now Black threatens ...♗xf3, which would leave him with a very superior pawn structure, and an excellent future. Nevertheless, White's best continuation is probably 10 h3 ♗xf3 11 gxf3 e6 12 f4, when Black has all the chances. Instead, White hopes to save himself with a clever tactic, but overlooks

the cleverer response, after which he is essentially lost.

| 10 | ♘bd2? | b5! |

But not 10...♘f4 11 ♗xf7+, when all is well with White. Now, however, White must either play 11 ♗xd5, which gives up his best minor piece, or take on a horribly cramped position. He chooses the latter.

| 11 | ♗b3 | ♘f4! |
| 12 | ♕f1 | ♕a5! |

This artificial-looking move is really quite effective, and forces the reply in order to avoid 13...♗xf3, which would paralyse White. By forcing 13 c3, Black makes the d3-square available to his pieces.

13	c3	♘d7!
14	♗c2!	♘xe5
15	♘d4!	

White plays in the best manner, but he is a pawn down and is just plain lost against proper play. Black's next move avoids any tricks beginning with ♘2b3, and prepares to exchange some minor pieces to ease the advance of his centre pawns.

15	...	♕c7!
16	♘e4	♘c4
17	h3	

I had expected 17 f3 followed by ♕f2 and 0-0, which is better than the text.

17	...	♗d7
18	g3	♘e6
19	♘f3	♘e5! *(D)*

To get rid of White's best placed piece and begin the advance of the

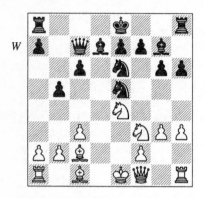

centre pawns. White must now reply 20 ②ed2, but, possibly discouraged by his poor position, he overlooks Black's full threats.

20	♕e2?	②xf3+
21	♕xf3	f5
22	②d2	0-0!

Now everything is clear! White dare not castle because of ...②g5 followed by ...f4. And, 23 ♗b3 is met simply by 23...♔h7.

23	②b3	c5
24	0-0	c4
25	②d4	

Losing another pawn, but one cannot blame White for rejecting 25 ②d2 ♗c6.

| 25 | ... | ②xd4 |
| | 0-1 | |

I gave the following 'if' move sequence: 26 cxd4 ♗c6 27 d5 ♗b7 after which the d5-pawn would soon be captured.

The essence of this game is that Black was willing to risk in the

opening, while White believed in the opening books. His 5 ②g5 was bad. After that he did not go into the losing complications of 7 c4 (which would still require much accurate play by Black), but chose an inferior position which he hoped would not be too bad. However, his 10 ②bd2 was a losing move, which allowed Black to expand decisively. He must have overlooked 10...b5. He had to play 10 h3 in order to have any chances, but here too Black has things all his way.

One Final Tidbit

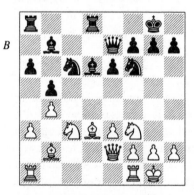

Rotlewi – Rubinstein
Lodz 1907

Finally, I cannot resist including a game fragment from one of the most beautiful and influential (on me) games ever played. In the diagram, we see the position of Rotlewi-Rubinstein, Lodz, 1907, after White's

15th move. Whereas in the initial position White has the advantage of half a move, here White has squandered his resources, and now has a development count of −2 since both his rooks are not yet developed. On the other hand, Black has a count of −1, and since it is his move, he is ahead in development by 1.5 in a rather symmetrical position. Let us see how this is turned to account.

15 ...   ♘e5!

Black plays **through** the centre, rather than occupying it with 15...e5, which would be effectively met by 16 ♘g5. Now the threat of ...♘xf3+ forces the exchange of knights, which gives the black pieces more scope.

16 ♘xe5   ♗xe5
17 f4

There is no need for this. The threat of 17...♗xh2+ 18 ♔xh2 ♕d6+ could safely be met by 17 ♖fd1 ♕c7 18 f4 and if 18...♗xc3, 19 ♖ac1 wins back the piece. However, White was clearly not up to the high level of tactics required to defend his position. Yet, the above is far from fatal.

17 ...   ♗c7
18 e4?

Putting another target in the centre for Black to shoot at. There is no hope of this leading to anything positive. Play should centre on the open files on the queenside and the invasion points c4 and c5. Now White's d4 is also weak.

18 ...   ♖ac8 *(D)*

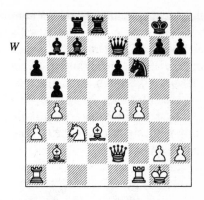

19 e5??

It was already difficult to find a defence to the threat of ...♗b6+ followed by ...♗d4. However, the move played, which drives the f6-knight to a better post, leaves the whole queenside undefended and opens up two major diagonals on to his own king, is hardly the answer.

19 ...   ♗b6+
20 ♔h1   ♘g4!
21 ♗e4

This must have been what White was counting on. If 21 ♕xg4, then 21...♖xd3 gives Black the two bishops and a vastly superior game. Now, however, the mating attack comes on like a thunderstorm, and the flimsy defensive structure that White has erected is exposed.

21 ...   ♕h4!
22 g3 *(D)*

After 22 h3 Black wins quickly with 22...♖xc3 23 ♗xc3 ♗xe4 24 ♕xe4 ♕g3! 25 hxg4 ♕h4#. There are other defences on move 23, which the student should work out for himself. The main point is that Black's pieces are all effective and supporting the attack, and White's are not placed well enough to counter this, so some of his pieces will become overloaded. But White hopes to gain time with his last move, attacking the queen.

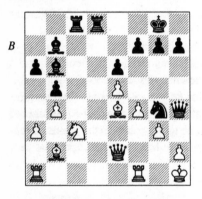

22 ...   Ixc3!!
23 gxh4   Id2!!
Now the full import of Black's play can be seen. There has been a systematic destruction of White's defensive set-up, and now the sole defender (the queen) is decoyed away from its primary duty of protecting the long diagonal h1-a8. There is no further hope now, so White goes down in flames in the most greedy way.

24 ♕xd2   ♗xe4+
25 ♕g2   Ih3!

0-1

There is no defence against the mate at h2. I can still remember the first time I played over this game, and how at about move 19 I felt that Black was about to embark on a terrific attack, and after 22 g3 'seeing' the sacrifice 22...Ixc3 followed by 23...Id2 instantaneously. How did that happen? It must have been an understanding of each of the defensive chunks and how the structure of these chunks could be shattered. This is dynamism at its best!!

8 Epilogue

It is now time to sum things up. I believe this book pushes forward the state-of-the-art of chess a good long way. We show how to:

a) Control the centre and make Black pay with small concessions if he wishes to compete there.

b) Develop the pieces harmoniously in order to achieve the above goal and still complete a constructive development plan that results from moving each piece just once.

We also show how to maintain the initiative with:

a) Crisp lines when the opponent challenges; or

b) Grabbing space and other advantages when he does not.

This is demonstrated across a variety of openings. The patterns are quite similar and some of my top-level chess colleagues, while not at all convinced of the correctness of all this, have been quick to point out certain features that appear again and again in **The System**. As you have probably also noticed, these are:

a) Playing f3 in order to control the e4-square;

b) Taking up the formation knight on c3, bishop on d3, knight on e2 in slow openings, where White must take a solid position upon which to build his advantage;

c) Delaying castling until it is absolutely clear where the king belongs;

d) Making a space-grab with b4 when there is no promising attack on the kingside or in the centre.

I started work on all this in 1949 after realizing the correctness of certain principles, and when it became clear to me that 1 d4 had to be the best first move. I have analysed and, perforce, played almost all openings that could arise in pursuing **The System**. I wish it were possible to say that the good ship **System** is now safely berthed in some friendly harbour. Unfortunately, that is not the case, and even though I hope to spend another 10 years on this endeavour, it is not realistic to assume it will be complete by then. However, computers will speed up this understanding with a little thoughtful programming.

Here, I would like to indulge in some philosophy. How could it be that a half-move lead in development could be transformed into a permanent advantage? This is only because it is at the start of the game where all territories are yet to be staked out. In the process of competing for some of these territories, Black must make some concessions, and thus there is an accretion of advantages. If the game were to start after each side had made several moves in a Pianissimo opening such as 1 e4 e5 2 ♘f3 ♘c6 3 ♗c4 ♗c5 4 ♘c3 ♘f6 5 d3 d6, then the advantage of having the first move has diminished greatly, and White can no longer count on it leading to any accretion.

So, one could ask how much of an advantage in time is necessary to have hopes of a permanent advantage? I am not really prepared to try to answer such a question. The closest I can come is from the games with Black where White strayed off the path too far, and Black got a lead in development of two or more tempi. If one also considers that three tempi are worth about a pawn, then one could say that an advantage of three tempi is very likely enough. We have seen many examples in this book where two tempi were very close to enough in a symmetrical position. Further, to try to evaluate everything in terms of tempi is insufficient. If there are already permanent advantages, then the tempi situation may be irrelevant. It is only when such advantages are still being jousted for, that the ability to force one's will on the opponent matters. And here comes the everlasting question: how far behind can one fall in development in order to 'secure' a permanent advantage?

Recently, a young Russian correspondence player named Umansky has won the 13th World Championship using exactly this style. He allows his opponents to grasp what appears to be a permanent advantage, but at the cost of two or three tempi, and then demolishes them. That this can be done in correspondence chess is very impressive since this is not the result of clever traps, but rather of solid play. The tempo balance is a very delicate quantity, and if managed correctly can lead to wonderful things.

Having summed up the positive, it behoves me to point out some of the current major deficiencies.

a) After the moves 1 d4 ♘f6 2 c4 d6 3 ♘c3 e5 it is still not clear what the correct **System** move is. On the one hand 4 dxe5 dxe5 5 ♕xd8+ ♔xd8 6 ♘f3 (or 6 ♗g5) is crying out to be played. However, neither I nor the whole rest of the world has been able to come up with any reliable advantage here. On the other hand, there is nothing wrong **System-wise** with 4 ♘f3 ♘bd7 5 e4, which gives White a space advantage at the cost of a somewhat awkward centre. Here, however, I am somewhat bothered by the application of the **Transposition Rule**. If the game had gone 3...♘bd7, White would not have played 4 ♘f3, but rather 4 e4 e5 5 ♘ge2 going into some good line of the Sämisch variation. 3...e5 is intended to force White's hand early, and succeeds in this. However, it is likely that ...♘bd7 is a major concession, since Black's queen's knight works best at c6 with pressure against the white centre. So one can take the view that after 3...e5 4 ♘f3 White is getting his concession in 4...♘bd7, and that 4 ♘f3 is correct. In support of this view, I can say that I have been playing this move, which relies on later queenside expansion. I have played some games like that, and they turned out to produce satisfactory prospects, but they did not feel like **System** games. However, it is also quite possible that 4 dxe5 is correct, but there are major problems in finding an effective continuation. One problem with this set-up is that the c4-pawn is weak and the d4-square in need of attention.

b) The Slav Defence, 1 d4 d5 2 c4 c6 3 ♘c3 ♘f6, was the earliest project I undertook under **System** guidelines. With the blocking of the best location for Black's queen's knight, I thought this should be the easiest nut to crack. But to date it still has not yielded its secrets as Alekhine also probed them (see p.5). I am basically convinced that 4 cxd5 cxd5 5 f3! is correct, with the likely follow-up 5...♘c6 6 e4 dxe4 7 d5 ♘e5 8 fxe4 e6. However, despite the fact that there are numerous violent attacking attempts here, and I have spent hundreds of hours on this, including much computer help, I have not been able to find any concrete advantage for White. Lately, I have looked at 4 f3?! dxc4 5 e4 b5 6 a4 b4 7 ♘a2 e5 8 ♗xc4 ♕xd4 9 ♕xd4 exd4 10 ♘e2 ♗c5 but have not found an advantageous continuation as yet.

c) The Nimzo-Indian is another unlikely-looking debut for Black. After 1 d4 ♘f6 2 c4 e6 3 ♘c3 ♗b4 Black seems to have only succeeded in annoying White temporarily, as a fly might an elephant. He has shut in his c8-bishop and now ventures forth alone with his good f8-bishop. How can this possibly be good? The moves 4 a3 ♗xc3+ 5 bxc3 c5 appear to be most thematic for both sides. However, now the thematic 6 f3 just does not work (again many hundreds of hours have been invested here) against 6...d5 7 cxd5 ♘xd5!.

These current failures might be upsetting to a less determined person, but I have seen the white play against the QGA rise from the ashes with the help of just one good idea (see Chapter 6, p.114). So help may be just around the corner on any or all these lines.

I am a little mindful of the caution expressed in the Introduction. Maybe some things will work according to **System** principles, and some not. However, I am too much of a scientist not to see a pattern in all this, and while chess is man-made, that does not prevent it from being susceptible to grand theories.

In any case, I have my hopes. I believe that if someone were to encode the **System** principles according to the guidelines given here, and include these in an evaluation function for a computer to apply at the end of variations to evaluate positions according to:

a) How well each move in the variation being analysed has corresponded to **System** principles. In particular, if material has been gained, how much has it cost **System-wise**. If a lot, then continue the analysis to see whether the material advantage will hold up.

b) The above should also be applied to 'positional' advantages such as leads in development, when all that has been accomplished is to get pieces out, but no cooperation or opponent targets exist.

c) Throwing out variations where some obvious violation of Principle takes place even if it wins a pawn.

d) And other things mentioned in this book, that will need to find their proper place in the scheme of things.

I have not been able to do this myself, because since 1985 my fortunes have been tied to the excellent chess machine, Hitech, which because of its very efficient operation did not allow the kinds of analyses required.

However, I am sure some reader of the above lines will be tempted to try this, and I wish him/her well. For instance, I think a reasonable project would be for a computer to play the white side of the QGD as shown in Chapter 4.

Finally, and most immodestly, I wish to compare this work with others that have come before.

Peter Gould and I decided that the proper name for this body of knowledge was indeed **The System** rather than titles such as Nimzowitsch's *My System* in which he acknowledges his own predilections while still contributing mightily to the understanding of chess. We wanted to claim that this is **The** theory of chess, not just **my** theory.

Philidor certainly got things off on the right foot with his writings on "Pawns are the Soul of Chess".

After that there were excellent ideas and books such as:
• Morphy discovering that one should complete one's development before attacking.
• Steinitz defining pawn weaknesses and how to avoid them.
• Rubinstein and the beginnings of an understanding of Dynamics, which Lasker clearly also understood to some degree.
• Capablanca and his notions of positional advantages.

- Nimzowitsch and his notions of blockade and outpost.
- Réti and the idea that the centre need not be occupied by pawns.
- Alekhine and his advanced notions of Dynamism, which for the first time included bold domination of the centre and aggressive intentions in the opening.
- Boleslavsky and how he transformed Réti's hypermodern ideas into a set of viable defensive systems for Black, and the excellent practitioner, David Bronstein, who showed the world how it all worked.
- Kmoch and his definitions of dynamic pawn tension.

Even to aspire to be among these greats may seem to many to be a vainglorious dream. I will await the judgement of time on this matter.

About the Author

Hans Berliner was born on January 27, 1929 in Berlin, Germany. In 1937 his family emigrated to the United States in order to escape Nazi persecution, and took up residence in Washington, D.C.

He learned chess at the age of 13, and it quickly became his main preoccupation. In 1949, he became a Master and won the District of Columbia (D.C.) Championship and also the Southern States Championship. He also tied for 2nd place with L. Evans in the perennially strong NY State Championship that year.

In national and regional competition, Berliner won the D.C. Championship five times, and won many other local and regional tournaments. These included the 1953 N.Y. State Championship (the first time ever won by a non-New Yorker), the 1956 Eastern States Open ahead of Rossolimo, Lombardy and Fischer, and the 1957 Champion of Champions tourney. He topped off a highly successful 1957 by finishing 5th in the US Invitational Championship behind Fischer, Reshevsky, Lombardy and Sherwin.

Berliner took up correspondence chess in 1955 in order to have more free time for his married life!?? He then won the Golden Knights tournament in 1955, 1956 and 1959; the only years he competed. By the time he retired from US Correspondence chess, he was rated almost a full category ahead of the next player. In 1959, he began playing International Correspondence chess. He won the 5th World Championship Final, which began in 1965, by the margin of 3 points, a record that exceeds any other performance by 2 points. After that, he retired from correspondence chess with a record of 94 wins, 1 loss, and 10 draws.

In 1975, he completed the Doctoral Degree in Computer Science at Carnegie Mellon University (CMU) in Pittsburgh. In 1979, a backgammon program that he had developed beat the reigning backgammon World Champion, Luigi Villa, by the score of 7-1. This was the first time a computer had beaten a World Champion at an acknowledged game of skill.

By 1984, he and a group of students designed, built and programmed the Chess Machine/Program Hitech. Hitech dominated the computer chess scene until late 1988. During this time it became a US Chess Federation Senior Master (top 50 players in US), won the Championship tourney of the state of Pennsylvania 3 times, and beat former US Chess Champion Arnold S. Denker in a match by the score of 3½-½.

For his various accomplishments, Dr Berliner is in the US Chess Hall of Fame, listed in Who's Who in America, a Fellow of the American Association for Artificial Intelligence. In 1998, Dr Berliner retired from academia to Florida.

Author's Address: 4000 N. Ocean Dr. # 1903, Riviera Beach, FL 33404.